D1557887

Monteverde

Monteverde

Science and Scientists in a Costa Rican Cloud Forest

Text and Photographs by

Sneed B. Collard III

FRANKLIN WATTS
A DIVISION OF GROLIER PUBLISHING
New York London Hong Kong Sydney
Danbury, Connecticut

To my stepfather, James Case,
with eternal thanks for keeping a roof over my head
and showing me my first tropical forest.

With love,
Sneed

Photographs ©: Michael & Patricia Fogden: 108; Richard LaVal: 100; Sneed B. Collard III: 13, 14, 17, 18, 20, 21, 22, 25, 29, 33, 34, 37, 39, 40, 43, 47, 48, 55, 56, 57, 58, 61, 64, 66, 71, 73, 74, 77, 78, 80, 83, 84, 89, 92, 103, 104, 105, 111, 112.
Insert #1 photographs ©: Sneed B. Collard III: 1, 2, 3, 4 top, 5, 6, 7, 8; Therese Frare: 4 bottom.
Insert #2 photographs ©: Michael & Patricia Fogden: 3, 4, 5; Sneed B. Collard III: 1, 2, 6, 7, 8.

Library of Congress Cataloging-in-Publication Data

Collard, Sneed B.
    Monteverde: science and scientists in a Costa Rican cloud forest / Sneed B. Collard III.
       p.   cm.— (Venture)
    Includes bibliographical references and index.
    Summary: The ecology of tropical forests that grow at high altitudes is described through the eyes of scientists who live and work at the Monteverde Cloud Forest Preserve in Costa Rica.
    ISBN 0-531-11369-8
    1. Cloud forest ecology—Research—Costa Rica—Reserva del Bosque Nuboso de Monteverde—Juvenile literature. 2. Cloud forests—Research—Costa Rica—Reserva del Bosque Nuboso de Monteverde—Juvenile literature. 3. Biologists—Biography—Juvenile literature. 4. Reserva del Bosque Nuboso de Monteverde (Costa Rica)—Juvenile literature. [1. Cloud forest ecology. 2. Cloud forests. 3. Monteverde Cloud Forest Preserve (Costa Rica)] I. Title
QH541.5.C63C64   1997
577.3—dc21
                                        96-49515
                                           CIP
                                          AC

Contents

Monteverde

Note to the Reader

This book was researched and photographed primarily during two visits to Monteverde, Costa Rica, during the dry and wet seasons of 1994. Most of the information in the book is derived from author interviews conducted in Costa Rica. Additional material was obtained from scientific research papers, books, and telephone interviews.

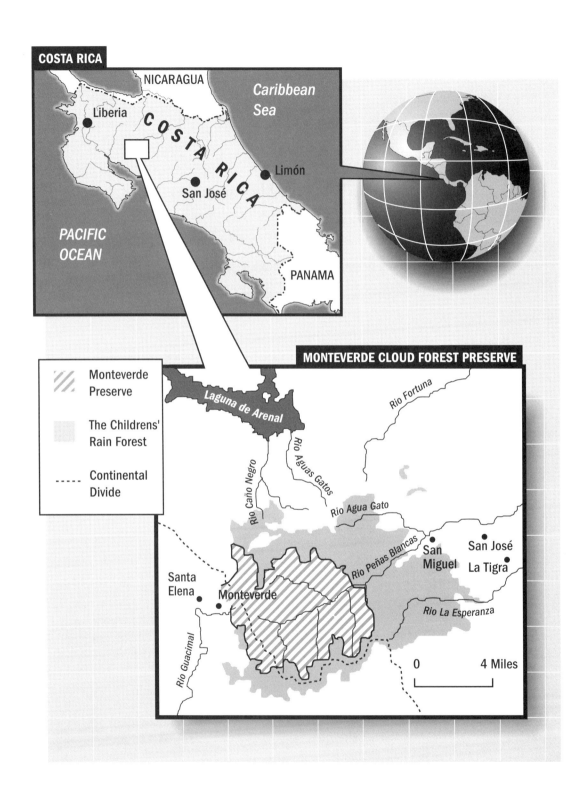

Life in the Clouds

People have paid a lot of attention to tropical forests in recent years. Most of us have heard about tropical rain forests, their animal life, and how they are being destroyed by logging, burning, mining, oil exploration, and other human activities. What most people don't realize is that our planet is home to many different types of tropical forests besides rain forests. This book explores a special kind of tropical forest that grows at high altitudes. Ecologists—biologists who study natural communities of plants and animals—refer to this kind of forest as a *tropical montane forest* or a *tropical cloud forest*.

Even though they aren't well known, tropical cloud forests are every bit as fascinating as tropical rain forests. Tropical cloud forests blanket high mountain areas in many parts of the world, from Central America to Africa, Asia to the Caribbean. Each tropical cloud forest is unique. Each survives under its own special weather conditions and harbors its own collection of plants and animals that are found nowhere else on earth. When scientists and other people talk about tropical cloud forests, however, one name stands out over all others: the Monteverde Cloud Forest Preserve.

The Monteverde Cloud Forest Preserve is part of a large, privately protected area in northwest Costa Rica. The Preserve straddles Costa

Rica's continental divide, right on top of a mountain range known as the Cordillera de Tilarán. Like a living quilt, several types of forests make up the Preserve, but a large tract of tropical cloud forest forms its heart.

The name Monteverde means "green mountain" in Spanish and is taken from a small Costa Rican village on the lower edge of the Preserve. Surprisingly, the town was founded not by Costa Ricans but by a group of North American Quakers, or Friends. The history of these Friends dates back to the 1940s, a time when young men were drafted to serve in the U.S. military forces or imprisoned for refusing to register for the draft. Quakers oppose all forms of violence, and they resisted being forced to serve in foreign wars. Many refused to register for the draft, and some were imprisoned as conscientious objectors. One group of Friends living in Fairhope, Alabama, decided to escape this persecution by finding a new country in which to live. They chose Costa Rica.

Costa Rica attracted the Friends because in 1948 the country had abolished its army—a philosophy that fit in with Quaker religious beliefs. Also, land was cheap in Costa Rica, a necessity for the Quaker immigrants, who were extremely poor. In 1950, a group of the Friends made an epic journey over land from Alabama to Costa Rica. The trip was a hard one. It was undertaken long before the Pan-American highway stitched together the countries of Central America. In one 30-kilometer (18-mile) stretch, the Quakers actually had to construct their own road through the wilderness. Despite these obstacles, the immigrants pushed on and reached Costa Rica after three months. After spending six months searching for a place to settle, they bought 1,500 hectares (3,750 acres) of land high in the Cordillera de Tilarán and founded the community of Monteverde.

With their knowledge of farming, the Quakers established a thriving community in Monteverde. Today, Monteverde is home to one of the most successful dairies in Central America. This has helped not only the Quakers,

Monteverde's plentiful rainfall allowed the original Quaker settlers to create a thriving dairy community.

but their neighboring Costa Ricans, who raise cows and supply the dairy with milk. Perhaps even more significant, the Quakers recognized that they depended on the cloud forest to provide them with a stable, clean water supply. To help protect this water supply, they set aside over one-third of their property as watershed and prohibited the cutting of trees there.

What the Quakers never predicted was that the tiny patch of forest they protected would one day become the core of an enormous tropical forest pre-

The Monteverde dairy produces some of the finest cheeses and other dairy products in Central America.

serve. They also never predicted that the forest would attract biologists from around the world. Over the next 30 years, hundreds of researchers journeyed to Monteverde to study the cloud forest and how to protect it. Many of these biologists have ended up settling in Monteverde while others have made it their second home, spending many months there each year. This book presents the cloud forest through the eyes of the scientists who live and work in Monteverde; it shares some of the many secrets they have uncovered.

Chapter One

The Forest in the Trees

A ripe fig comes whizzing out of the tree and smacks into the mud next to Bob Lawton's feet.

"Ah, missed!" Bob shouts at his attackers—a troop of white-faced capuchin monkeys. But the monkeys aren't through with their target practice. Soon, other figs follow the first, striking uncomfortably close to their human targets. Bob isn't fazed. He seems to be enjoying the show. "They're all up there in the upper crown," he says, peering into the tree. "They got the lay on us, but at least they're not trying to pee on us. Sometimes they do."

While his enthusiasm toward the monkeys is obvious, Bob is even more interested in the trees and the forest in which the monkeys live. Bob is an ecologist who has spent the last 20 years studying the trees and other plants of Monteverde. As with many biologists, Bob's interest in nature began at an early age, while growing up in Tallahassee, Florida.

"I was always interested in biology and stuff as a kid," he explains. "Exploring swamps and woods and things. Then, when I was 16, I drove down to Panama with my parents. A couple years later I returned with a friend. We worked for biologists for a month in exchange for room and board, and then we bummed through Central America. We slept in ditches, hitchhiked, you know, all that kind of stuff. I did that off and on in college and became a botany major. By then, I was thoroughly hooked on the tropics."

Unlike many other biologists, however, Bob wasn't interested in tropical forests solely as a home for animals and plants. Instead, he wanted to understand how the forests worked and how the trees and other plants "made their livings." In 1976, he drove through Central America with his wife, Marcy, who is also a biologist and was interested in studying birds. They were looking for a place where both of them could work, and they settled on Monteverde. The mountain community offered brown jays for Marcy to study (see chapter four) and plenty of undisturbed forest for Bob to dive into.

For his study area, Bob chose an 8.8-hectare (22-acre) plot of forest on top of the continental divide, in an area known as the Brillante Gap. This is the wettest part of the cloud forest. Almost every day, the area is bathed in clouds. The clouds originate in the westerly trade winds blowing off of the Caribbean Sea. As these winds strike land, they climb up the eastern slope of Costa Rica's mountains and the air in them begins to cool. As the air cools, moisture is "squeezed" out of it. By the time the winds reach the continental divide, they are heavily laden with clouds that soak the ridge tops with rain and mist.

Water, however, is not the only force that shapes Bob's study site. Growing directly atop the divide sits a unique type of forest called the *elfin forest*. The trees in the elfin forest are small, reaching no more than 5 to 10 meters tall (16 to 33 feet). Their small height is an adaptation not to water but to the trade winds that constantly blow. Even on calm days, wind gusts up to 60 kilometers (38 miles) per hour are common. During winter storms, called *temporales*, gales exceeding 150 kilometers (94 miles) per hour pound the divide. The trees in the elfin forest survive this assault by growing low to the ground.

The Brillante Gap is where trade winds from the Caribbean Sea cross the continental divide, bringing with them the moisture that waters the unique cloud forest community.

They also develop trunks and branches that are much stronger, with denser wood, than trees growing in more sheltered sites.

GETTIN' ALONG WITH THE NEIGHBORS

When Bob began his work, he had many questions about the elfin forest and about the taller forest farther down the slope in his study site. His most funda-

mental question related to the *diversity*, or number, of species that lived together in the forest.

Unlike most temperate forests, tropical forests are usually packed with many different species living in close proximity. Monteverde is no exception. More than 2,500 species or kinds of plants have been identified from the Preserve—almost as many as live in the entire state of Florida, an area that is thousands of times larger.

One basic question Bob and other ecologists ask about tropical forests is "How can so many different species live all in the same place?" Bob particularly has wondered if different kinds of trees survive as neighbors by doing different things.

"In the tropics," Bob explains, "it is simply not the case that basically a tree is a tree and it grows, flowers, and produces seeds and there you are. Part of the beauty of the tropics is that it's not merely that there are more kinds of trees per acre—more oaks, more hickories, more of the *same*. It's that the trees are doing things down here that they don't do in the temperate zone."

As an example, Bob points to the life history of *Ficus crassiuscula*, the tree the white-faced monkeys were sitting in. *Ficus crassiuscula* belongs to a group of trees called "strangler figs." Strangler figs are common in tropical forests throughout the world and are known for their macabre lifestyle. Stranglers don't start their lives sprouting in the ground as other trees do. They sprout in the tops of other trees, where their seeds are dropped by fruit-eating birds, bats, monkeys, and other animals. After a strangler seed germinates, the

---

Ficus crassiuscula *has evolved a lifestyle that is bizarre, even by strangler fig standards.*

Ficus crassiuscula *figs provide food for a variety of cloud forest creatures, from monkeys to bats.*

young strangler plant sends a leaf-filled stalk up toward the sky while a slender root snakes down the trunk of the strangler's *host* tree to the soil below.

As the tree grows, it sends up more branches skyward and more roots toward the ground. The strangler's leafy canopy shades the leaves of its host tree, robbing it of the sunlight it needs to make food. Meanwhile, the fig's roots totally encase the host's trunk and, bit by bit, cut off the living tissues that the host needs to survive. The host cannot escape the strangler's grip and eventually dies, leaving the strangler standing tall and healthy in the forest.

The strangler's lifestyle sounds cruel, but by sprouting in the tops of other trees, strangler fig trees obtain light and space that may be difficult to find on the dark, crowded forest floor. Despite this advantage, many fig seedlings are doomed to die because they are dropped in places where they cannot survive. Even if their seeds happen to land on the branch of another tree, that branch may not offer enough sunlight, water, or nutrients for the young fig to grow.

Enter *Ficus crassiuscula.*

Bob Lawton and his graduate student Jim Daniels have discovered

The viney stage of Ficus crassiuscula *is what gives the tree a "second chance" to survive in the cloud forest.*

THOUGHTS FROM A BIOLOGY STUDENT

Field research usually isn't a biologist's only job. In addition to conducting research, Bob Lawton teaches classes at the University of Alabama, where he is a professor. Bob also mentors students in the art of biology. One of those students is Jim Daniels, who is working for his Ph.D., or doctorate, degree.

Jim readily admits that he isn't a typical Ph.D. student. Born and raised in Huntsville, Alabama, he never fueled a burning desire to join academia.

"I had a good time as an undergraduate," Jim recalls, sitting in front of the A-frame house he rents while working in Monteverde. "I had not been very scholastic. But then I ran into Bob Lawton, and he kind of saved me. He showed me that you could have a good time and get a college degree at the same time."

Jim had done some field work for Bob while still an undergraduate at the University of Alabama. When he graduated, the only thing Jim knew was that he wanted to do something different. Bob told him about $250 grants available to students from the Alabama Academy of Sciences. The grants were used to support research.

Jim Daniels is one of many graduate students who have conducted their graduate research at Monteverde.

Jim asked what he could do with such a grant and Bob told him about the strangler fig Ficus crassiuscula.

"He described it," Jim remembers. "And I said 'Neat. Does it strangle one tree more than others?' And Bob said, 'Hey, that's a really good question.' And away we went."

Jim came to Monteverde with Bob in 1987. He and Bob designed a study that showed Ficus crassiuscula does indeed seem to "strangle" some kinds of trees more than others. Jim used the data he collected to earn his master's degree.

For his Ph.D. work, Jim shifted focus. Instead of fig trees, he decided to study epiphylls—plants that grow on leaves of other plants. Jim hasn't drawn any earth-shattering conclusions about epiphylls, but he has developed some perspective about tropical biology and being a biologist.

"We really don't know enough about what goes on in the forest," he says. "Many people will tell you they do, but I don't think we ever will know completely what's going on. We might be able to chip away at some questions, but the fig trees or the epiphylls are very little pieces.

"But it's something to do," he continues. "And it's entertaining. That's the big thing for me. I get bored pretty quickly and I like biological research because it's a completion. You get a question and you figure out how you're going to answer it."

Does he like working in the tropics?

"Yeah, I do and I don't," he muses. "There are some things I miss in the States. It's hard to get around here. I don't have a vehicle so I end up walking everywhere. Sometimes, I really wish I could just get in my car and go get a pizza.

"On the other hand, what's really neat here is that you always run into something new. In fact, my last time in the study area, I ran into a huge land snail I hadn't seen before. It had a three-inch shell. I've been working here six years on and off and I've never seen it before. That's a lot of fun."

that *Ficus crassiuscula* "gives" itself a second chance to survive, a chance that other stranglers don't have. Instead of growing into a tree immediately, *Ficus crassiuscula* first develops into a sprawling viny plant or bush. It sends out tendrils that reach out to different parts of a host tree's trunk and branches. After several years, a young fig tree trunk begins to grow, as with other strangler figs. The difference, though, is that the new tree trunk can start from any part of the vine. If the place where the seed was dropped is not a suitable "nursery," the fig tree can start growing from another place several meters away. In a way, *Ficus crassiuscula* "chooses" the best place to grow, a strategy that improves its chances of survival.

FILLING THE GAPS

By studying the life histories of *Ficus crassiuscula* and other trees, Bob has discovered some clues about how so many different tree species are able to survive as close neighbors. To find out more, Bob has also been studying disturbances in the forest. Disturbances are events that alter the normal fabric of the forest. The most common types of disturbances happen when wind or landslides knock down trees. These disturbances create clearings, or *gaps*, in the forest canopy.

Ecologists are very interested in gaps because they allow light to reach the forest floor and may allow certain trees to grow that would never get a chance otherwise. In parts of the cloud forest where there are no gaps, almost no sunlight reaches the forest floor. Instead, it is all captured by the tall adult trees that form the forest canopy. Some tree seeds may sprout under these shady conditions, but even if they do, they aren't likely to grow into adult trees because of the shortage of sunlight energy.

"In looking at some species," Bob explains, "I've got trees I tagged as

Bob Lawton has been tracking gaps in the cloud forest since the 1970s.

saplings back in 1984 that are the same size today, 12 years later. They are sitting there for decades in the dark forest understory. They don't seem to be making good progress in the shaded conditions they're under, so my guess is that it will require some sort of increase in light to enable them to grow up and reach the canopy."

To find out if he is right, Bob visits Monteverde every summer and does an extensive survey of his study area. In each survey, he records which gaps are present, how large they are, and what species are growing in them. The surveys are very difficult. The constant presence of clouds keeps every centimeter of ground slippery wet. Vines, roots, and branches form dense thickets of vegetation that make footing difficult if not impossible. "After you fall three or four times," Bob says with a hearty laugh, "you know it's time to call it a day."

After years of conducting his surveys, however, Bob has collected data that clearly show disturbances are necessary for at least some forest species. One of Bob's favorite study trees, *Didymopanax pittieri*, is a good example. This tree is *shade intolerant*. It can grow only in well-lit conditions, such as those created by gaps. Without forest gaps, young *Didymopanax pittieri* would never receive enough sunlight to grow, and ultimately, the species would disappear.

EASY QUESTIONS, DIFFICULT ANSWERS

Eventually, Bob hopes that his data on gaps and plant life histories will provide a good picture of how different species survive in the forest and how the forest functions as a whole. One thing Bob has learned already is that the maintenance of a forest is an incredibly complex process. Bob found this out when he decided to look into the role of disturbance in the windswept elfin forest at the top of his study site.

"Since it's so much windier on the ridge," Bob explains, "it seemed reasonable for me to believe that the reason trees are so short there is because the frequency of disturbance is higher. Sort of a 'plucking the weeds' kind of effect. If you pluck the trees rapidly enough, they never have time to grow large. And so a simple-minded question is: 'Is the rate of disturbance, the tree turnover rate, higher in these dwarf forests than in the taller forests?' It sounds easy to answer. The question is simple and in principle, all you've got to do is check and find out whether gaps are created more frequently up on the ridges.

"However, having said it's simple," Bob continues, "it turns out to be a real chore. Every year, you go out and walk through the study area and find all the gaps and map them and sketch them and stuff like this. And what it shows is that there's no easy answer to your question. The rates of disturbance aren't dramatically different in the elfin forest than in the tall forest. In other words, the level of disturbance is not what makes the elfin forest short, but it took us a lot of work to find that out."

FOR WHAT IT'S WORTH

Despite the difficulty of his work, Bob remains enthusiastic about studying the forest and searching for keys to its mysteries. After watching him slip and slide through his study site year after year, one may wonder why he bothers.

Bob replies, "Well, some of the biggest reasons come from the old Joni Mitchell line. 'You don't know what you've got 'til it's gone.' We literally can't evaluate the biological assets that we have on earth until we know what they are. We also can't know what we could lose by using the land foolishly. Those are two major reasons to study tropical forests.

"Also, in a practical management sense," he continues, "if you don't understand how the trees in the forest behave, your hopes of commercially managing the forest are down the tubes. That's why monoculture forestry—where people plant only one kind of tree—is so popular. If you know and understand slash pines, for instance, you can just clear everything else and plant slash pines. But working with a more complex forest without destroying it is much more difficult. You need to know and understand a lot more. And while the elfin forest isn't being used for timber or that sort of thing, the kinds of knowledge we are gathering here are the kinds that will be required for intelligent forest management in the future."

In addition to the practical aspects of his work, Bob doesn't hide the fact that he just plain finds satisfaction in working in the cloud forest. When asked what his favorite thing about the cloud forest is, he responds, "I enjoy the exuberance of it. There are few terrestrial habitats that are as crowded with plant life. Like a coral reef, you practically swim through a cloud forest. You've got trees growing on trees, and bushes growing on the trees that are growing on trees, and vines growing on the bushes that are growing on the trees that are growing on the trees—and stuff plastered on the sides as well! It's, it's—Ah! If you like natural history, you'll never be the same after coming here."

THE FOREST PHARMACY

Tropical forest plants and animals have long been a source of important products for people. These range from rubber and other raw materials to food and prescription drugs. One recent survey identified more than 40 major prescription drugs that are derived from tropical forest plants and animals. These include everything from anti-malarial drugs to medicines that treat cancer. Bob Lawton is one of many scientists who keep an eye out for plants that may be useful to people. One thing that attracted his attention was the wonderfully fragrant flowers of a cloud forest tree called Guettarda poasana.

Bob admits that his first interest in the flowers wasn't entirely altruistic. Wondering what made the flowers smell so good, he asked himself, "Can we get rich on the perfume industry?" Bob put the problem to an organic chemist, Will Setzer, at the University of Alabama in Huntsville. Will extracted the fragrant essential oils in the flowers to locate the source of their wonderful smell. Disappointingly, Will discovered that the flowers' fragrance came from alcohols that were already readily available in the chemical industry.

So much for getting rich.

But Bob's interest in the flowers didn't stop with their fragrance. Bob, Setzer, cell biologist Deb Moriarity, and several students did some quick tests with the flowers' oils and discovered that the oils also killed a variety of microbes. These included bacteria and fungi, such as yeasts. Bob and his colleagues found that even small traces of one of the flowers' alcohols, cinnamyl alcohol, had a remarkable ability to prevent yeasts from growing.

This made perfect sense to Bob. In order to be fertilized, most flowers must attract insects or

The fallen flowers of Guettarda poasana cast a delicious smell through many parts of the cloud forest. Guettarda is just one of thousands of tropical forest plants which may contain chemicals useful to humans.

other animals to pollinate them. However yeasts, which are very common in the tropics, can quickly destroy the nectar that attracts these animals. Bob deduced that flowers that made their own "nectar preservative" would have an advantage over flowers that did not. Ultimately, natural selection would favor the "preserved" flowers and eliminate flowers without preservatives.

Guettarda isn't the only cloud forest plant Bob's team has tested for useful properties. They have also investigated the leaves of two species of Dendropanax trees. The team found that chemicals in the leaves killed viruses and certain kinds of cancer cells. It isn't certain whether the chemicals in Dendropanax and Guettarda will ever find their way into local drug or grocery stores, but they provide a compelling reason to protect cloud forests and other tropical forests. With the number of tropical plants in the world and the many chemicals that they produce, it is likely that cures for AIDS and many other diseases are growing out there, waiting to be discovered. Protecting the "tropical forest pharmacy" may, in the long run, be one of the best ways we have of protecting ourselves.

Chapter Two

Science in the Sky

"Right over there, I nearly saw my husband *die*," Nalini Nadkarni says, pointing to the top of a large tree. As she speaks, she is perched 23 meters (75 feet) above the forest floor, casually straddling the branch of a neighboring strangler fig tree.

"It was horrible," Nalini recalls. "We were being filmed for a documentary called *The Infinite Voyage* and Jack was with another member of the film crew. He was climbing that tree over there and suddenly the cord that tied his Jumar to his belt failed (see Field Notes: "Reaching the Top"). It undid. And so he fell and I saw him go over backwards and went 'AAAAAAH!'

"He fell about 15 feet before his safety line stopped him, but meanwhile the film crew was filming him as he went down and it was just incredibly traumatic. We laughed about it later because they actually kept filming him. I can't believe they did that. They thought it was great footage!"

Fortunately, her husband's brush with death was the only serious accident Nalini or any of her co-workers has experienced during the past 15 years—a remarkable statistic given that Nalini has climbed thousands of rain forest trees, from the Pacific Northwest to Papua New Guinea to

Central America. Nalini concedes that she's been lucky, but she also has enormous confidence in her equipment and climbing skills. It's a good thing, because a huge part of Nalini's life is spent up in the forest canopy. The reason?

Epiphytes.

LOOKING UP

Nalini was born and grew up in Bethesda, Maryland. A "terminal tomboy," she spent many of her happiest hours in a "super-treehouse" her father built for her. Something about being in the trees stuck with her. Though she had a strong interest in dance growing up, she decided to pursue her other passion, biology, as a profession. She graduated with honors from Brown University and went on to earn her Ph.D. at the University of Washington in Seattle.

It was while she was doing her graduate research that she first developed an interest in *epiphytes*. Epiphytes are plants that live on top of other plants. They obtain support—but not nutrients or water—from their host plants. Epiphytes cover the trees of Monteverde and include such well-known plants as orchids, bromeliads, mosses, and philodendrons.

"The basic idea I started out with was kind of born here in Monteverde," Nalini recalls, sitting high in one of her favorite fig trees. "I first came down to Costa Rica to take an OTS course.[1]

"I just started walking through the forest here and looked up at all these epiphytes in the trees. I thought, 'Whatever is going on in this forest, something important is happening with these epiphytes.' I asked myself what that thing was and what the epiphytes were doing."

---

[1] OTS stands for Organization of Tropical Studies, a consortium of colleges and universities dedicated to educating students in tropical biology.

Tropical montane, or cloud, forests only exist where trade winds carry warm, moist air into the mountains.

A strangler fig's host tree often rots away, exposing the hollow, living trunk of the adult strangler.

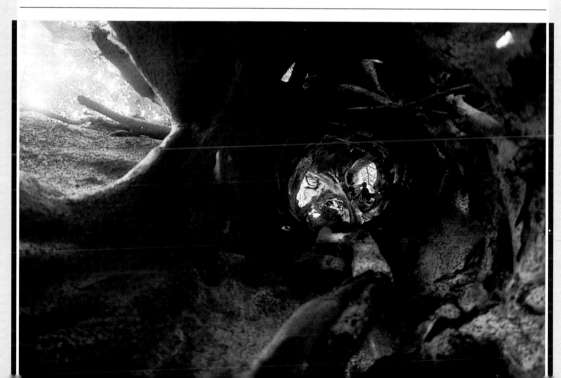

Approximately 300 kinds of strangler fig trees live in the world's tropics. Their lifestyle sounds cruel, but the trees' fruit provides sustenance for thousands of tropical forest animals.

Bob Lawton often has to slip and slide his way through the elfin forest in his study area.

Rare in drier ecosystems, primitive plants called liverworts thrive in the mist-drenched cloud forest understory.

Of the 28,000 known species of epiphytes, 20,000 are orchids. Most orchids are small plants that can easily be overlooked, but some produce dazzling red or pink flowers that attract their hummingbird pollinators.

With the help of climbing ropes and bright-yellow "Jumar" ascenders, Nalini Nadkarni has climbed thousands of trees in her efforts to understand the ecology of epiphytes.

Piper plants are one of many epiphytes that are useful to cloud forest animals. The plants' long, white inflorescences are a favorite food for some bats.

The woolly opossum is one of countless nocturnal animals in the Monteverde area. This opossum is almost completely arboreal, feeding on fruits in forest trees.

At night, tarantulas sit and wait outside their burrow entrances for unsuspecting insects to happen by.

One of many kinds of katydids that take the nighttime stage.

Almost impossible to detect during the day, walkingsticks are active nocturnal foragers.

The common vampire bat is one of 43 kinds of bats that live in and around Monteverde. Despite popular myths, the bats pose little threat to people, preferring to feed on the blood of sleeping cows and deer.

Richard Laval shows students first-hand what remarkable creatures bats are.

When she returned to Washington, she asked her advisors at the university what they could tell her about the epiphytes. She discovered that very little was known about the plants' role in the forest community. For her Ph.D.

work, Nalini decided to try to figure out how much nitrogen, phosphorus, and other nutrients were wrapped up in the bodies of the epiphytes compared with the rest of the forest. She started her work in the windswept elfin forest at Monteverde, but her advisors urged her not to focus on only tropical ecosystems. Instead, they encouraged her to compare Monteverde's cloud forest with the rain forests of Washington and the Pacific Northwest. It was this comparison that led to a startling discovery.

Rare in many temperate forests, epiphytes often cover cloud forest trees.

REACHING THE TOP

One reason so little is known about epiphytes and other aspects of the tropical forest canopy is because until recently, very few people were able to reach the canopy to observe and study it. In the 1970s, however, biologists began using rock-climbing and mountaineering equipment to reach the top of the forest.

Nalini Nadkarni learned basic tree-climbing techniques from another tropical biologist, Donald Perry. Perry had pioneered the use of climbing ropes and other equipment in tree-climbing during the 1970s. Over the years, however, Nalini has also come up with her own inventions to help her work in the forest canopy.

Nalini's first step in climbing a tree is to shoot a fishing line over a large branch of the tree. To help her do this, she invented the "Master-Caster," a powerful slingshot attached to a metal rod with a fishing reel. Aiming at a branch, Nalini shoots the line with a weight on the end of it. She rarely hits her target on the first try. Sometimes it takes her over an hour—or even an entire day—to place the line exactly where she wants it. Once the line is over the branch, she uses it to pull

After Nalini uses her "Master-Caster" to shoot fishing line over a tree branch, she uses the line to pull parachute chord and, in turn, climbing rope over the tree branch.

heavier parachute cord over the branch. Nalini then ties climbing rope to the parachute cord and pulls that over the branch as well. She anchors the climbing rope to the trunk of a nearby tree and then prepares to climb.

To climb, Nalini attaches a pair of "Jumar" ascenders to both the climbing rope and to a climbing harness around her waist. Jumar ascenders are special clamps that grab onto a rope and slide up but not down. They allow Nalini to "inchworm" her way up the climbing rope without touching or bumping into the trunk of the tree. This prevents her from damaging epiphytes growing there and also keeps her from being stung or bitten by any trunk-dwelling animals.

Using the Jumar ascenders, Nalini can scale a 25-meter (82-foot) tree in less than a minute. When she reaches her branch of choice, she secures her harness to a safety line in the top of the tree and then she is ready to work.

Advanced climbing techniques have allowed Nalini and other canopy researchers unprecedented freedom to explore the canopy. Nalini has come up with other innovations that enable her to spend long periods of time in the trees. In the mid-1980s, Nalini began pulling a collapsible aluminum cot up with her when she climbed. The cot was originally designed for rock climbers, but Nalini found it was a good, portable way to "settle in" to the canopy for long periods of time. The cot came with a rain tent that kept her dry even during tropical rain showers—something she and her colleague Teri Matelson found useful during their study of how birds use epiphytes.

Over the years, Nalini has taken hundreds of people up in the trees with her, including her two children, Gus and Erika. She has great trust in her equipment, but despite years of experience climbing trees, she maintains a healthy respect for the dangers of her work. She encourages her fellow climbers to do likewise. "I always ask people who want to go up if they're afraid," she says. "If they say 'yes,' then I know they'll do OK. I want a little fear; that means they'll be safe."

To measure epiphyte nutrients, Nalini climbed trees and began stripping the mosses, orchids, and other epiphytes from the branches they were growing on. Then she dried and weighed these samples so she could compare the weight of nutrients in epiphytes to those in the leaves and branches of trees. One day, while working in a big-leaf maple tree in Washington State, Nalini encountered a surprise. As she began stripping off a layer of moss and the soil and dead material that had gathered beneath it, she suddenly found a maple tree root. Nalini, of course, had seen plenty of maple roots before, but always growing *into* the forest floor. This root was growing into the mat of epiphytes 13 meters (40 feet) *above* the forest floor!

Nalini had never before heard of this sort of root, which she dubbed a *canopy* root. At the same time, she figured someone must know something about it. When she talked to her advisors and read up on epiphytes, however, she discovered that no one had ever heard of such a thing. Nalini quickly climbed other kinds of trees to see if they also grew canopy roots. Not all of them did, but she discovered canopy roots growing from three other species of common Washington forest trees.

Nalini's discovery attracted worldwide attention. Results of her work appeared in prestigious journals such as *Science, Ecology, Brenesia,* and *Biotropica.* She also became the subject of articles in popular magazines, including *Glamour* and even *Highlights for Children.* For Nalini, however, canopy roots were not the end of her journey of discovery. They were the beginning.

THE FOREST BANK ACCOUNT

One of the first questions Nalini asked herself was, "What were the canopy roots doing up there?" Obviously, the roots were absorbing nutrients and perhaps water that the epiphytes had accumulated. But how important were the epiphytes to the tree's survival? More important, how did epiphytes affect the flow of nutrients through the entire forest?

"Basically, you start looking at a forest like a bank," Nalini explains. "In the bank, there are certain inputs of nutrients, or 'money,' that you can think of as deposits. There are certain checking or savings accounts where nutrients get deposited in the system for shorter or longer periods of time. And there are withdrawals—ways that nutrients can come out of the bank. And so what people who study nutrient cycling do is they are being bankers. They're looking at inputs, storage, and outputs —as well as how the nutrients get transferred from place to place.

"What's interesting,"

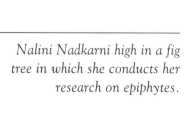

Nalini Nadkarni high in a fig tree in which she conducts her research on epiphytes.

Nalini continues, "is that different banks, or different accounts in banks, have different amounts of nutrients that come in, come out, and are stored. And so when I started looking into this, my overall goal was to say, 'I want to understand the bank account of nutrients in this forest, and I want to understand in particular how epiphytes enter into that. Are they accumulating lots of nutrients? Are the nutrients getting stuck up there forever? Or are the epiphytes transferring them to other parts of the ecosystem?'"

Ironically, Nalini's questions about banks applied not only to her theories on nutrient cycles but to the issue of how she was going to afford answering her questions. To pay for her research, she began applying for grants from the National Science Foundation and other sources.

"I got turned down a number of times," she remembers, "because the canopy was sort of viewed as insignificant. It wasn't major enough. Also, I was young and you know, I was much too ambitious in my proposals, as all young people are. Anyway, after three go-rounds, my grant got funded, but the grant committee said, 'OK, just start very basic. Don't go up and do all these experiments and so forth. Just start with the basic questions, because really, what you're doing is sort of nineteenth-century biology. No one has described in any sort of basic way what the epiphytic community or environment is like in a tropical cloud forest.'"

EPIPHYTES 101

Nalini followed the grant committee's advice—sort of. With funding in hand, she set out to both describe the epiphytic community *and* answer her questions about nutrient cycling in the cloud forest. She assembled a team of biologists and students and came to Monteverde to go to work. She set up a four-hectare plot—about the size of eight football fields—in the tall forest on the leeward, or drier, side of the continental divide. Then, she began conducting a variety

In one of her nutrient studies, Nalini discovered that dead leaves don't stay up in the canopy very long. To figure this out, she placed leaves on special "Astro Mats" up in the trees and checked them at regular intervals.

of experiments that measured the amount of nutrients coming into the system and going out of it.

The epiphytes, Nalini has found, play a key role in regulating the nutrients available to the forest. Many epiphytes are especially adapted to grab nutrients from dust in the air or from water droplets in passing clouds. Members of one class of epiphytes, *tank bromeliads*, grow a special cuplike structure, or tank, in their center. This tank not only holds rainwater for the plants to

WHAT'S IN A MAT?

"Guess how long ago that bare spot was cleared?" asks Nalini Nadkarni, pointing to the branch of a large fig tree. The branch is covered by a thick mat of epiphytes, all except for a one-meter (three-foot) section near the trunk where the epiphytes have been removed. In contrast to the rest of the branch, the bare patch supports only a thin layer of lichens, mosses and other green "fuzz." A casual observer might guess the bare patch had been cleared only a year ago, maybe two at the most. The answer, however, turns out to be five years and it provides an important insight into epiphytes and the forest in general.

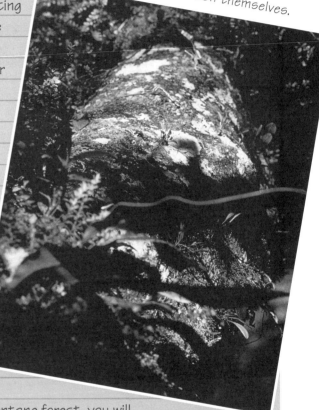

Five years after this spot on a branch was cleared, the epiphytes have only just begun to re-establish themselves.

If you look at the trees in a montane forest, you will quickly observe that not all of them are loaded with epiphytes. Young trees often have few epiphytes, while large, older trees often seem smothered in them. To better understand where epiphytes seemed to be growing and why, Nalini flew a tree surgeon to Costa Rica from Florida in the summer of 1992. Nalini directed the tree surgeon to cut and carefully lower branches from several trees of different ages and kinds. Then, she and her associates removed and weighed the epiphytes growing on every part of the trees.

Nalini discovered that small trees had less than one-tenth of one percent of all epiphytes in the forest where she worked. The bulk of the epiphytes were found in the large, mature trees. Nalini also found that 85 percent of the epiphytes grew on the inner, bigger branches of the large trees, while only 3 percent grew on the outer branches and 9 percent on the trunk.

Nalini's results and her other observations suggest that epiphytes don't appear overnight. They also point out that epiphyte mats are far from simple. "What the scenario seems to be," Nalini explains, "is that these epiphyte mats are quite complex. You get the substrate of the older mats, which is like a humus or soil up there. It is formed from rotting leaves and roots. On top of that, you get these mosses and small plants called liverworts, which together are like a pillow and a sponge. And on top of that, you get higher vascular plants like shrubs and ferns and herbs and that sort of thing.

"And what we're guessing or hypothesizing is that the larger vascular plants, such as ferns and orchids, give the whole mat its structure. Their roots keep the mat intact and attached to the tree branch. The larger plants might also be very important in serving as a surface area. Cloud mists condense against the leaves of these plants, and then the water gets funneled down to the moss mat. For their part, the mosses and liverworts seem to be the ones which are really good at slurping in the mist and rainfall. They remove certain nutrients like nitrates and release waste products like ammonia, which become available to other plants and animals."

The overall result is that the mat functions as its own ecosystem, one that can take a very long time to develop. This is fascinating in its own right, but it also has important implications for conservation. It demonstrates that when people cut down an old-growth forest, we lose a lot more than just the trees. We also lose a whole set of organisms that survive only in older forests and, of course, the benefits that those organisms provide.

use but also captures nutrients in the form of dust, fallen leaves, insects, and bird droppings. Other epiphytes have equally marvelous means of obtaining nutrients.

But the epiphytes aren't the only ones that benefit from these nutrients. They also pass the nutrients on to the rest of the forest. Many cloud forest tree species, like the ones in Washington State, use canopy roots to grab nutrients from the mats of epiphytes that accumulate on their branches. Epiphytes also drop dead leaves onto the forest floor. When these leaves decompose, they become part of the forest's "nutrient bank account." Sometimes, whole branches full of epiphytes crash down to the forest floor and die, likewise passing their nutrients on to the other forest species.

Nalini's findings are especially important because nutrients in tropical forests may be especially hard to come by. Many people look at all the plants growing in a cloud forest or rain forest and think it is an extremely fertile place. Because of all the rain, however, nutrients—such as phosphorus and nitrogen—may quickly wash out of forest soils and become lost to the forest ecosystem. The survival of many plant species may in part depend on the nutrients that epiphytes grab out of the atmosphere and pass on to the rest of the forest.

Ultimately, what Nalini is trying to do with her data on epiphytes is to construct a nutrient-cycling model of the whole forest. The model will tell her where nutrients come from, where they are stored, how they are transferred within the ecosystem, and finally, how they leave the system.

"The problem," Nalini says, "is that you can't isolate anything in the forest. And that is both the hardship of being an ecologist and the joy of being an ecologist." You can't really understand epiphytes, Nalini explains, without understanding the rest of the cloud forest. As a result, she and her team have been conducting other studies to figure out how the forest ecosystem works.

EPIPHYTE BIRDS, EPIPHYTE BUGS

In one project conducted with research associate Teri Matelson, Nalini examined the use of epiphytes by birds. She especially enjoyed that project because it allowed her and Teri to stay up in the tree canopy for six hours a day watching birds and other wildlife. From the study, Nalini learned that epiphytes are a major resource for birds living in the cloud forest. Of 71 species of birds that

Many epiphytes provide food and other resources to cloud forest animals. This spotted flower of the epiphyte Capanea grandiflora *is one of many flowers which provide nectar and pollen to hummingbirds and bats.*

visited their study area during the project, 33 species visited epiphytes for food. Others came to find nesting materials and shelter. These birds included some of Monteverde's most dazzling species: hummingbirds, tanagers, toucanets, and many others.

In another study, Nalini worked with her husband Jack Longino. Jack, also a biologist, studies ants and other insects. In their joint study, Jack and Nalini wanted to compare the numbers of invertebrates (animals without backbones) in the canopy versus the forest floor. Together, Jack and Nalini collected and identified invertebrates from the epiphytic mats of eight different trees. Then they collected invertebrates in the leaf layer beneath each of the trees.

One thing the study showed them was that the same groups of invertebrates live up in the epiphytes as live on the forest floor. These included mites, beetles, ants, springtails, and pill bug–type animals called amphipods and isopods. In the canopy, however, the numbers of these animals were lower than they were on the ground. Nalini is not sure why, but it may be because more wind blows through the canopy. The wind tends to dry out the epiphytic mats, making it a harsher environment for invertebrates to live in.

Another interesting result of this study was that even though the same groups of invertebrates lived in the epiphytes and on the ground, the actual species were almost completely different. This helps demonstrate that epiphytes are extremely important in maintaining *biodiversity*—the total number of species on our planet.

COUNTING EARTH'S NATURAL TREASURES

Studies of tree canopies have dramatically altered estimates of how many kinds of animals, plants, and other species live on our planet. The new estimates arose from the work of another tropical forest ecologist—and colleague of Nalini's—named Terry Erwin. In the early 1970s, Erwin investigated how many beetle species lived in the tops of trees in Peru. He laid out huge tarps under the trees and then sprayed insecticide up into the canopy. His study may seem crude, but the results revolutionized the scientific world. The sheer number of beetles that fell out of the trees startled Erwin. Even more amazing was the fact that most of the beetles were entirely new species, ones that had never been described by scientists. What's more, Erwin discovered that if he collected insects from different trees even a short distance away, he got almost completely different sets of beetle species!

Because of Erwin's work and studies that followed it, scientists have raised their estimates of biodiversity on our planet. Scientists once estimated there might be between five and ten million different species on earth. Now, estimates range as high as 30 million.

Epiphytes are clearly the homes to many of these unknown species. Epiphytes themselves also greatly contribute to species totals. Twenty-eight thousand species of vascular, or higher, plants are epiphytic—one out of every ten vascular plant species on earth. Nalini, her husband, and other tropical biologists are just beginning to unlock the mysteries of these plants. As they continue their work exploring the treetops of Monteverde and other tropical forests, they are sure to discover many more secrets and treasures in the world above our heads.

Chapter Three

They Only Come Out at Night

Many people come to the cloud forest and other tropical forests expecting to be surrounded by colorful, exciting animals. When they take their first walk through a place such as Monteverde, however, they are often disappointed. "Where are all the animals?" they ask themselves. "Where are the jaguars? The sloths? The monkeys?" Although these animals live in Monteverde and in other tropical forests, it is a rare event to see them. Why? Because tropical animals are masters of "hide and seek."

Hiding can be a huge advantage to a tropical forest creature. Most tropical forests are dangerous places, full of predators that are constantly searching for a meal. Hiding can prevent an animal from becoming dinner for one of its enemies. On the flip side, if you are a predator, hiding can also help you catch the animals you would like to eat.

Tropical forest animals hide in several ways. *Camouflage* is one. Camouflage colors and shapes help animals blend in with their surroundings and may provide advantages to both predators and prey. A *nocturnal* lifestyle is an even more common way to hide.

Where is it? This frog's masterful camouflage helps protect it from enemies on the forest floor. (Hint: the frog is in the center of the photograph, pointed to the left.)

NIGHTSTALKING

Nocturnal animals remain still and inactive during the day, reducing their chances of being noticed by predators. At night, nocturnal animals "wake up" to hunt, mate, and forage.

In Monteverde, the appearance of nocturnal animals is dramatic. During the day, you may walk along a forest trail and see only a scattering of insects,

Katydids are some of the noisiest cloud forest creatures. They also have some of the most remarkable camouflage. Their wing coverings look just like a leaf, and their legs and antennae resemble brown sticks.

frogs, and other creatures. Walk along the same forest at night, however, and you'll be in for a surprise.

The sounds are the first things that fill your senses. A barrage of chirping, whining, buzzing, croaking, clicking, and popping assaults your ears as soon as the sun goes down. Flick on your flashlight and you'll discover some of the musicians that create this spectacular symphony. Insects are the most common nighttime animals in the cloud forest, as they are in any forest. Sitting out on leaves or crawling across the forest floor, a startling carnival of moths, wasps, crickets, beetles, ants, and other insects actively forages or hunts under the protection of darkness.

Because of their enormous sizes and amazing shapes, katydids and walkingsticks often steal the show from other nocturnal insects. Katydids are a group of large insects known for their loud, whining sounds, which drench the cloud forest night with sound. Katydids may resemble grasshoppers or crickets, but the most startling look almost exactly like leaves.

Equally dramatic are the walkingsticks, or stick insects. Walkingsticks are the longest insects on earth. Some varieties in Asia grow up to 32 centimeters (13 inches) long. Fourteen or 15 centimeters (about six inches) is a more common length in Monteverde. As their name implies, walkingsticks resemble twigs or sticks. During the day, they stay "stick still." At night, they quietly climb about in search of the leaves and other plant material that they eat.

Insects, however, are not the only nocturnal animals you'll see in the cloud forest. If you are very quiet, you might sneak up on a tarantula waiting outside its burrow for a juicy cockroach to come along. Flash your beam into the bushes and you might surprise a small pig-like mammal called a paca foraging for fallen fruits or invertebrates. Owls live in the cloud forest, as do woolly opossums with big ears and piercing eyes. Of all the cloud forest's nocturnal creatures, however, some of the most fascinating are ones that you may never see—that is, not unless you accompany mammalogist Richard LaVal.

CAPED CRUSADER

Richard LaVal moved to Monteverde with his wife Meg in 1980. Since then, they have done many different things to earn a living: raised cattle, farmed,

A CAMOUFLAGED ENIGMA

While thousands of camouflaged creatures live in the forests of Monteverde, some attract special scientific attention. One of these is a treehopper called Umbonia ataliba. Umbonia is a small, beautiful animal. About as long as a thumbnail, it is adorned with camouflage red-and-green colors and a "thorn" that helps protect it from birds, lizards, and other predators. Its interest to scientists, however, centers on another characteristic: sex.

Umbonia is one of the few creatures on earth in which mating occurs almost exclusively between brothers and sisters. Such pairings, known as "inbreeding," are rare among other animals and are strictly taboo in human society—with good reason. Mating among family members greatly increases the chances of birth defects, diseases, and other characteristics that reduce survival among offspring. Why, then, does inbreeding occur in Umbonia?

Biologist Karen Masters has spent several years studying this issue. Living in Monteverde with her biologist husband Alan and twin sons Cameron and Adrian, she has carried out a number of experiments that seek to determine whether inbreeding offers any advantages to Umbonia. Although she has not finished analyzing her results, she thinks she has some clues.

One advantage to mating with a brother or sister, Karen explains, is that it can save you a lot of energy. Umbonia are born in broods of about 90 females and males. They hatch as larvae and go through four life stages before turning into adults. Once they are adults, however, they live for only a few weeks. Going off to search for a mate during this period might take a lot of energy and use up the treehopper's precious time. By mating with siblings that are right next to them, the treehoppers make the best use of the energy and time they have available.

A second advantage to mating close to home is that it may reduce the treehopper's chances of being eaten. Umbonia adults don't move much, and they may be extremely hard to detect by predators. If, however, they flew around searching for mates, they might greatly increase their chances of becoming lunch for a hungry bird or lizard.

What about the problem of disease or birth defects? For populations of animals that have begun to inbreed relatively recently, this is sure to be a hazard, but perhaps only at first. Karen and other biologists believe that if a population survives an extended period of inbreeding, most of the undesirable characteristics of the organism may be "weeded out." What's left are individuals that are basically all the same but have characteristics that are very successful for the specific conditions in which they live. Karen's experiments have indicated that a female Umbonia that mates with a sibling actually produces more eggs than a female that mates with a nonfamily member. This provides some evidence that inbreeding is more successful for Umbonia than "outbreeding."

Of course, no system is perfect. The down side of inbreeding is that Umbonia probably has less genetic variation than other species. If Umbonia's environment changes significantly, it is possible that none of the treehoppers will have the genetic features it takes to survive. For Umbonia, however, the risk seems to have paid off—as long as we humans continue to care about and protect the forests where it lives.

taught classes, rented horses, and for Meg, sold her artwork. Richard, though, is best recognized for the name that thousands of students and tourists have assigned to him: the bat man.

Richard has loved bats ever since he was a child growing up in Missouri, but his professional interest in them began when he entered graduate school in mammalogy at Louisiana State University.

"In the first graduate course I took in mammalogy," Richard recalls, "we were assigned to do a research project, and I chose bats because I had always liked them.

"When I was a child," he continues, "no one had even studied bats. No one knew anything about bats, and everyone was scared of them, superstitious about them. They thought bats carried rabies and believed a lot of old wives' tales. But I thought bats were beautiful animals. I couldn't understand why people thought all these bad things about them, so it didn't bother me at all to study bats. In fact, I discovered real quick that not much research had been done on bats at that time—back in the 1960s—so anything I could do would be a contribution."

From Louisiana, Richard was drawn to the tropics not only because of the high number of bats living there, but because of the incredible diversity of tropical plants and animals in general. He stumbled upon Monteverde while conducting a research project during the early 1970s. The project's objective was to answer the question, "Do insect-eating animals reproduce when insects are most abundant?" The answer turned out to be yes, and it gave Richard an extended opportunity to learn about spiders, frogs, lizards, and, of course, bats in their natural habitats.

Interestingly, Richard and Meg did not move to Costa Rica to pursue biology. Instead, they were searching for a better quality of life for themselves and their family. Bats, however, have continued to be a major theme in

Richard's life. Several times a year, groups of students come to Monteverde to take classes in tropical biology. These students are joined by a steady stream of teacher groups, naturalists, and tourists who are eager to visit and learn about the cloud forest.

Richard frequently gives lectures to these groups of people about bats and other animals of the cloud forest. One night a week or so, he also takes a few lucky people "bat-netting."

GETTING "BAT READY"

On one particular night in July, Richard meets with a group of teachers from Oregon. They have agreed to rendezvous in a drier part of Monteverde known as Bajo del Tigre, a patch of forest that was named after a jaguar that lived there in the 1940s.

Richard arrives early in Bajo del Tigre, his tall frame dressed in his usual bat-netting uniform: worn jeans, a long-sleeved blue work shirt, and a green caver's helmet complete with headlamp. Working quickly and efficiently, he begins setting up four "mist nets" he has brought with him. The nets have about the same mesh as a tennis net, but are made from very thin filament that is too small for the bats to detect. Richard stretches the nets across a trail, looping the ends of the nets to poles, which he in turn ties to trees. The last glow of daylight begins to fade as he finishes his work. Within moments, the teachers arrive.

"Now what we try to do is sample the kinds of bats that fly where our nets are," Richard explains to the teachers. "We've set our mist nets right over a trail, and clearly, not all bats fly where these nets are set. In fact, most of them do not. On a really good night, though, we might catch as many as 10 different kinds out of the 43 species that live here in Monteverde. By the way,

43 is about the same number that lives in the whole U.S. and Canada combined. And there's a lot more than that that live in the lowlands of Costa Rica, about 110 species in the whole country.

"Basically," Richard continues, "as you move north to south, you get more kinds of bats. The country that has the most species is Peru, which is just barely south of the equator. But for the size of the country, I don't know if there's any other country that has more than Costa Rica. Even Peru has only 153 species, which isn't many more than Costa Rica.

"So, as I said," Richard resumes, "there's the same number of bats here as in the States. But there's a lot more scientific families represented here, especially in the lowlands of Costa Rica, where there's ten different families of bats. In North America, there's only three scientific families of bats and in most of North America, there's just one, the Vespertilionidae or 'mouse-eared bats.'"

"How about picture-taking?" one of the teachers inquires. "Is that going to freak them out?"

"Well, let's put it this way," Richard responds. "Everybody does it. I've been netting in some of these places for more than 20 years and have been catching the same number of bats as I always have and in the same places. So, it can't be bothering them too much."

"But," Richard says with a smile, "now, I have to tell you my T-rex story."

As the teachers listen intently, Richard compares a bat's experience being captured to a person being captured by a giant *Tyrannosaurus rex*. Instead of eating the person, however, the giant dinosaur simply studies the human, poking it here and there, trying to learn more about it. After it's finished, the dinosaur sets the amazed person gently back on the ground, leaving him free to continue his life in peace.

When Richard is done with his story, the teachers clap and laugh delightedly. Then, it is time to get to work.

CLOSE ENCOUNTERS OF A BAT KIND

Taking three teachers with him, Richard walks up a trail to check the nets. Sure enough, Richard's headlight illuminates two bats struggling in the mesh of the first net. Kneeling down, Richard gently grabs hold of one bat and, like a surgeon, carefully extracts the animal from its trap. He places the bat in one of two cloth bags attached to his waist. The bags are orange with little black bats printed on them and were made in Monteverde especially for Richard. Richard then removes the second bat and places it in a bag. After that, he

Mist nets designed to catch birds also provide an effective way to capture bats without hurting them.

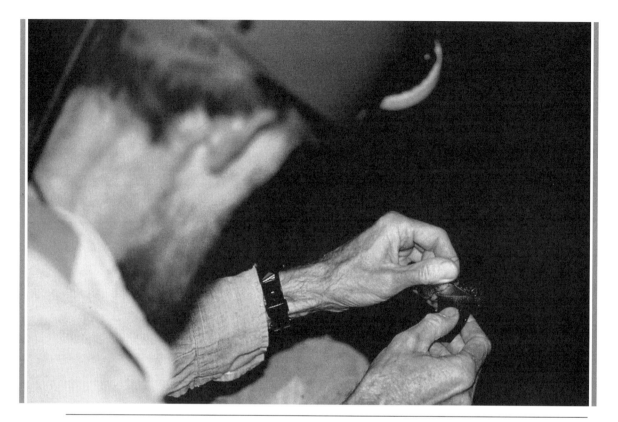

Richard LaVal carefully removes a bat from a net. Each year, Richard takes hundreds of teachers, students, and tourists "bat netting" to help educate them about bats.

checks the remaining three nets, each of which contains at least one bat. With his waist bags full, Richard walks back to the main group of teachers to introduce them to his living treasures.

Reaching into his bag, Richard first pulls out a kind of leaf-nosed bat. The teachers let out a chorus of "oohs" and "ahs."

"This is one of the six species of nectar-feeding bats that we get here," Richard explains. "See its long little tongue? These bats are like humming-

This is one of more than 25 species of leaf-nosed bats that live in the Monteverde area.

birds. They come to flowers, they hover in front of the flower, they stick their tongue down the flower, the whole works. But they go to different kinds of flowers than hummingbirds. They go to flowers that bloom at night. Typical 'bat flowers' are green. Bright red flowers are not going to attract anyone at night, right? Bat flowers are green with a strong odor. One of the flower species here smells exactly like a skunk. Some of 'em smell good, but that just happens to be a very strong odor that carries a long way, and that's important for bats."

One of the teachers asks if bats can see very well.

Richard explains that many bats have extremely good vision and can see as well as any nighttime animal. For fruit bats, vision appears to be a very important sense. Bats, however, have two other important senses. One is smell. The other is hearing. Hearing is vitally important to most bats, because they use *echolocation* to find their way around. Echolocation is a kind of sonar —the bats emit small, high-pitched noises and then listen for the echo of those noises to figure out what's around them.

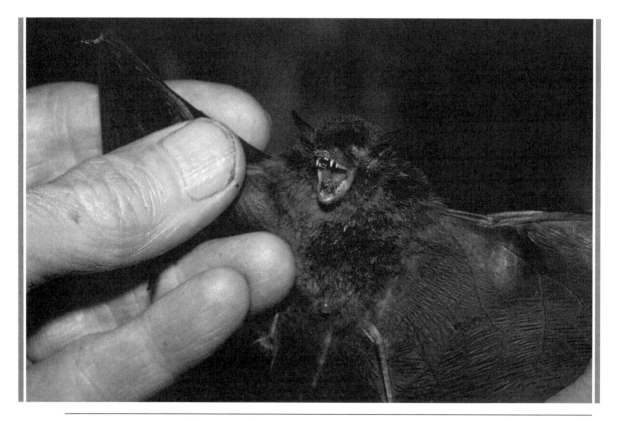

An insect-eating bat displays the remains of its last catch.

"Echolocation helps bats forage through a lot of clutter, like flying through all this stuff," Richard says, gesturing toward the thick growth of plants surrounding the teachers. "Bats can fly around in this even in pitch darkness." He adds that echolocation seems to be especially important for insectivorous bats, those that hunt mosquitoes and other insects.

Returning his attention to the bat he is holding, Richard stretches out its wing. The wing is surprisingly thin, and the light from Richard's headlamp beam glows through it. Richard explains that if the wing is damaged so the bat can't fly, it usually dies from starvation. "These guys eat two to three times their weight every night in nectar or fruit," Richard says. "Insectivorous bats don't eat that much, because it's not necessary. Insects are a lot more nutritious than fruit or nectar."

Richard also points out how short the bat's tail is. He contrasts this with another bat that he pulls out of his bag. The second bat is an insectivorous bat.

"Now, let me show you some of the major differences between this insectivorous bat and all these others. There's this big membrane down here with the tail in the middle of it. That's her rudder that she uses to make those big turns that bats can make when they're chasing bugs. She can also cup the membrane under her and that helps her to catch an insect. If she misses with her mouth, she can cup her tail membrane and grab an insect in that."

Examining the bat carefully, Richard adds, "She appears to be pregnant. She's running a little late, too. In this species, the first young of the year or 'pups' are born in June. So she's either having her first pup or she's already had her first and she's pregnant with her second. Most of them around here have two babies a year."

Another bat in Richard's bag—a Toltec fruit bat—is also pregnant. "Now this one has already raised one baby this year," Richard explains. "And that baby would have been born sometime in April, probably early April. The reason I know that is the teats are located under the armpits, and if I look under her armpits, I see a patch of more or less bare skin there. You can see the teat. The hair has grown back a bit, but if she had a baby now, it would be all bare and her nipples would be sticking out. By the way, when the babies are born, they weigh about a third of the mother's weight. Because they are so big, they're very well developed when they are born and in six weeks, they're ready to fly."

AN EXPERIENCE TO REMEMBER

Richard keeps pulling bats out of his bag and tells his audience a little about each one. The highlight of the evening comes when Richard gives each person an opportunity to hold a live bat in his or her bare hands. Before passing the fruit bat and other bats around, Richard carefully demonstrates how to safely handle the animals.

"Now watch how I do this," he says. "These little bats are pretty delicate and you just handle them for what they are. You pick up a bat with your middle finger and thumb and the next finger at the elbows. When you hold him like that he can't do a thing. And then you pass him into your other hand like this, over the edge of the hand so if he feels like biting you, he's probably not going to encounter your hand right off.

"Now, the thing to remember," Richard continues, "is that these are wild animals. I can't predict what they're going to do. If one feels like biting you, it will. Now, he's not big enough to do any serious damage. He probably can't even break your skin. But, the thing you don't want to do is jerk suddenly if he bites at you because you might break his front teeth. And he'd probably starve to death, because they use their front teeth, which are long and sharp, to pick fruit with."

The unique experience of holding a bat turns many bat haters into bat lovers.

One by one, each person in the group handles a bat. The bats are surprisingly warm and cuddly wrapped in one's hand. The rapid heartbeats of the bats can be felt against the skin of the people's fingers. Some of the bats struggle to free themselves, but many are quite passive, calmly accepting the petting and fawning that their large mammalian relatives bestow upon them. Fears about bats vanish as the bats are passed around. Even a woman who for years has been terrified of bats musters up her courage to hold one. Her face immediately softens as she realizes the delicate nature and beauty of the animal she is holding.

When a bat appears to be growing fussy or seems particularly uncomfortable being handled, releasing it is not a problem. Richard or one of the teachers simply tosses the bat into the air and with a quick flash of its wings, it darts off into the forest. The teachers sigh appreciatively each time one of the animals flies away. For the bat, its brief captivity has been no more than a brief—and probably uncomfortable—experience. For the humans, it has created a memory and an understanding that will last a lifetime.

Chapter Four

Stars in the Clouds

If you ever get the chance to visit Monteverde, especially between the months of January and July, you are likely to run into crowds of tourists with their cameras and binoculars pointed toward the tops of trees. These people are stargazers, but the stars they seek aren't in outer space. They are perched on branches in and among the forest canopy. These stars are tropical birds.

Monteverde—indeed all of Costa Rica—is a bird-watcher's paradise. Costa Rica is less than half the size of Ohio, but it contains more bird species than all of North America. More than 850 species of birds have been observed in Costa Rica. Six hundred of these are permanent residents, and more than 200 others migrate each year to nest in North America and as far away as New Zealand, Siberia, and Antarctica.

More than 300 bird species can be observed in and around Monteverde itself. Hiking along a trail, you're liable to encounter a colorful blue-crowned motmot perched on a low branch, waiting to swoop down on a tasty snake or lizard. Two dozen different kinds of hummingbirds of many sizes and shapes may zoom past you. Some feed on nectar while others pursue insects and spiders.

One spectacle you'll see in Monteverde is mixed feeding flocks.

Birds are one of Monteverde's major attractions. Here, a newborn hummingbird sits well-camouflaged in its teacup-size nest.

These flocks of birds may appear suddenly along a trail and contain many different, often dazzling, species. The birds seem to poke frantically among bark, leaves, and branches looking for insects, lizards, and other morsels. As suddenly as they appear, they are gone again, off to investigate a different patch of forest.

Mixed flocks occur in many tropical forests. In Monteverde, more than 60 species of birds have been observed in these flocks, including common bush tanagers, three-striped warblers, nightingale thrushes, wood creepers, and black-faced solitaires. Ecologists aren't certain why mixed flocks exist, but foraging together may help members of the flock find food and detect predators.

Though the mixed flocks and everyday birds of Monteverde are enough to keep a bird-watcher occupied for years, two feathered stars attract special attention. They are the three-wattled bellbird and the resplendent quetzal.

BONK!

Bellbirds can be difficult to see, but they state their presence loud and clear. Starting about March, some of the birds arrive in Monteverde from the lowlands, where they have been feeding. The

BUTTERFLYIN' THROUGH

Although birds get more attention, Monteverde's butterflies draw their share of oohs and ahs from visitors. More than 500 different butterfly species have been identified in Monteverde. They range from spectacular iridescent blue morpho butterflies as big as a person's hand to a host of tiny brown flutterers that barely attract attention.

Although tourists focus on butterflies for their looks, scientists study them for different reasons. Biologist Bill Haber has lived and worked in Monteverde for more than 20 years. He is an expert on many of Monteverde's plants and animals but has a particular interest in butterflies and how they migrate. Between 1984 and 1986, Bill spent hundreds of hours catching butterflies and identifying them. He discovered that more than half of the butterflies found in Monteverde aren't permanent residents. They are migrating through.

Different butterfly species migrate at different times and to different places. Some butterflies live in lowland

Many lowland species of butterflies escape the harsh dry season by migrating to or through Monteverde.

forests on the Pacific Ocean side of the mountains. These forests endure a harsh dry season every year, and during this time, many of the butterflies migrate to Monteverde or to the Atlantic Ocean side of the mountains, where it is wetter. Other butterflies spend most of the year on the Atlantic side and fly up to Monteverde during its rainy season.

Different species of butterflies probably migrate in response to different conditions. Some may migrate because of the dry weather. Others may move because of predators or because their food plants stop flowering. Remarkably, many of the butterflies do not complete a full migration cycle. Some lowland forest butterflies fly to the Atlantic side, lay their eggs, and die. Their offspring then grow up and return to the

Pacific side, where they also reproduce and die. How these butterflies know where to go and when are two of the many mysteries that confront butterfly biologists.

One group of migrating butterflies that has attracted special attention is the ithomiine "clearwing" butterflies. Clearwing butterflies are a favorite among butterfly enthusiasts because of their transparent wings. These wings allow the butterflies to "disappear" against any background and are thought to help protect the butterflies from predators.

Clearwing butterflies are also armed with a potent chemical defense system. Male butterflies obtain powerful chemicals called pyrrolizidine alkaloids from the flowers they feed upon. These chemicals make the butterflies taste bad to birds. The males also use the chemicals as pheromones to attract female butterflies.

Interestingly, female ithomiines don't get their chemicals by feeding on flowers. They obtain them from male butterflies during mating. During mating season, the female mates with many different males. This allows her to obtain plenty of sperm and plenty of chemicals. The chemicals protect her from being eaten, and she also passes some on to her eggs, a process that may protect them from being attacked by beetles and fungi.

One hitch for the butterflies is that in Monteverde, the flowers that contain the alkaloids do not flower in large numbers all year long. Biologist Alan Masters, the husband of Karen Masters, discovered that for large parts of the year, clearwings and their relatives contain few or no chemicals that would protect them from predators. Does this mean it is more dangerous for an individual butterfly during these times of the year? Not necessarily. Alan found that the time when butterflies are least protected coincides with the time when they are most abundant. This means that the chances of an individual butterfly being eaten may actually be less than usual, because predators have more butterflies to choose from.

males announce their return with a loud metallic "BONK!" that can be heard up to 1.6 kilometers (one mile) away.

From any given spot in the forest, it's not unusual to hear four or five bellbirds bonking at the same time from different treetops. The main purpose of the bonking is to attract females. The bonk advertises that a male is ready to mate. Once a female draws near, the male's three flashy "wattles" and distinct brown-and-white coloration also indicate that the male is mature and may help convince a female that a certain male is the one for her.

Female bellbirds are much more subtle than their noisy male counterparts. They "dress" in rather drab olive and yellow feathers and go about their business without bonking. After a female mates, she receives no assistance from the male. She builds the nest and raises the young completely on her own. This is in striking contrast to the other star of the Monteverde bird community, the resplendent quetzal.

STAR POWER

The resplendent quetzal is without a doubt the most popular attraction in Monteverde. Between 40,000 and 50,000 people visit Monteverde each year. If you asked each of them what they would most like to see, the majority would answer, "the quetzal."

The quetzal is a member of the trogon family. It cannot be mistaken for any other bird. Its dark green wing coverts (feathers that cover the wings) shimmer like wet green leaves when the quetzal is quietly perched in the forest canopy. When it swoops to a nearby branch to pluck a wild fig or avocado fruit, however, it exposes its brilliant red breast and showy white, black, and green tail feathers. Although both male and female quetzals are impressive, the male's adornment is particularly breathtaking. Four long, emerald tail-coverts extend up to 25 centimeters (10 inches) beyond the bird's rump, and a glittering green "crown" completes the royal regalia for this stunning creature.

The quetzals' range extends from southern Mexico to western Panama. The birds have been sought after since the Aztecs captured them for their feathers more than a thousand years ago. The feathers were used to decorate warriors' costumes and were considered a precious commodity, along with gold and turquoise. It is believed that on more than one occasion, Aztec rulers even waged war on neighboring states to gain access to the feathers.

Today, the quetzal is appreciated more for its beauty than as a commodity. It is the national bird of Guatemala and even lends its name to that country's currency. Its picture has appeared on hundreds of travel brochures, conservation magazines, and books about rain forests, earning the quetzal a reputation as the most spectacular bird in the New World.

Part of the bird's mystique lies in the fact that it lives only in high, forested mountains. This has been fortunate for the people of Monteverde. Recently, much of the community's income has come from tourists longing to see the green-and-red flash of the quetzal in the cloud forest trees. Until the late 1970s, however, scientists knew very little about the quetzal. The bird's natural history had been described in the 1940s and some additional work on conservation of the bird had been done in the late 1960s and early 1970s. When Nat Wheelwright arrived in Monteverde in 1979, however, almost nothing was known about the relationship between the birds and their food sources.

BIRD-CURIOUS

As with many scientists who work in Costa Rica, Nat was first introduced to Monteverde while taking a course in tropical ecology given by the Organization for Tropical Studies. His interest in birds and nature, however, began much earlier.

"I grew up in Massachusetts and was sort of a kid bird-watcher," Nat explains. "Then, I got to that age when I realized it was not cool to be a bird-watcher. If I wanted to be socially acceptable, I had to hide that side of me, so I kind of went into remission. Then, in late high school, I realized, 'Who cares? It's O.K. to like birds.' If people didn't like me the way I was, that was their problem."

Nat decided to pursue his natural history interests while attending Yale University. During his senior year, he went to his ornithology professor and asked how he might travel to South America. His professor asked Nat if he'd like a job helping out with some studies examining how closely certain tropical bird species were related to each other. Nat jumped at the chance and for the next year traveled through Colombia and Ecuador collecting bird blood samples. Afterward, Nat returned to the United States and began graduate school at the University of Washington. In the summer of 1978, he took the OTS course in Costa Rica and eventually decided to do his Ph.D. research in Monteverde.

A MARRIAGE OF CONVENIENCE

Nat had many questions about tropical forests, but he was especially interested in the relationship between quetzals and their primary food, the fruits of the plant family *Lauraceae*, also known as wild avocados. Quetzals and avocado plants appeared to have a *mutualistic* relationship, one in which both organisms benefit from each other. The quetzals fed heavily on the large wild avocado fruits and in return, the birds seemed to help the plants by spreading their seeds to different parts of the forest.

Mutualistic relationships are fairly common in nature. One of the most well-known is the case in which flowers provide nectar to butterflies and the butterflies spread the flowers' pollen to other flowers. Although this and other mutualistic relationships have been well studied, no one had ever looked closely at the relationship between the quetzal and the avocado trees. Nat wondered whether quetzals really depended on the avocado fruits to survive and whether the avocado trees really needed the quetzal to spread their seeds through the forest.

Between 1979 and 1982, Nat followed quetzals and watched what they were eating. He also observed their courtship, movements, and care of their young. Nat discovered many things about the quetzal during this time.

One discovery he made

Nat Wheelwright counts wild avocado fruits in his efforts to understand the relationship between fruit-eating birds and the trees in which they feed.

was that the quetzal did indeed specialize in eating avocado fruits. Nat found that although quetzals ate fruit from 17 different plant families, more than 80 percent of their diet consisted of wild avocado fruits. What's more, quetzals "followed" the lauraceous fruits, migrating up and down the mountains as the fruits ripened in different places.

The quetzal-avocado relationship seemed even stronger when it came to the birds' breeding cycle. Nat found that spring and summer—the times when quetzals bred—were also the times when wild avocado fruits were most abundant. As with many bird species, male and female quetzals work together to raise their young. They pick out a dead tree trunk and with their beaks, carve out a nest hole. When the young hatch out, the parents at first bring them a variety of food, including walkingsticks, lizards, beetles, grasshoppers, and snails. Nat observed, however, that within a few days, the adults begin feeding their young primarily on wild avocado fruits. He concluded that by having their babies when these fruits are most abundant, the quetzals increase the chances that their young will survive to adulthood.

THE FLIP SIDE

Nat's observations confirmed half of the mutualistic relationship between the quetzal and the avocado plants. The quetzals seemed to benefit from the plants. But did the plants benefit from the quetzals? Before Nat studied the relationship, everyone assumed that the answer was "yes." They assumed that, like butterflies pollinating flowers, the quetzals did a good job spreading the avocado seeds around the forest and thus "repaid" the avocado plants for feeding them. Surprisingly, the relationship didn't turn out to be that simple.

"The analogy with a pollination system," Nat explains, "seemed to break down with the quetzal and the wild avocado plants. Although seed dispersal seems similar to pollination, it is quite a different ball game. I expected to see a high-quality type of seed dispersal by the quetzals, one in which the birds would drop many of the seeds in favorable spots for new trees to grow. But it turned out that the quetzal's seed dispersal was in many respects quite poor. The birds tended to drop the seeds where a lot of other animals would eat and destroy them."

Upon closer inspection, the "friendly" mutualistic relationship also seemed to break down as far as the avocado plants were concerned. In one

Though not as large as those sold in grocery stores, wild avocado fruits are large enough that only a few kinds of birds can swallow them.

Wild avocado fruits are "the pits." While tasty and attractive from the outside, the avocado "package" is almost all seed and little fruit.

study, Nat measured how many calories the avocado fruits contained and how many fruits the quetzals were able to eat. He came up with a surprising conclusion: the avocado plants weren't simply feeding the birds. In a way, they were "tricking" them.

Nat discovered that avocado fruits alone don't contain enough nutrition for quetzals to survive. Why not? To eat avocado fruits, quetzals must swallow them whole. Unfortunately, the fruits are so large that a bird can only swallow two or three of them at a time. Afterward, it must wait about half an hour before the fruits are digested and the bird can regurgitate the large avocado seeds. Nat calculated that even if the birds ate avocado fruits as quickly as possible, the fruits still would not provide enough calories for the birds to survive. This is an advantage for the avocado plants. It means that they can invest less energy and nutrients into making their fruits, yet still "convince" the quetzals to eat their fruits and disperse their seeds. However, it also means that quetzals can't rely solely on avocado trees to survive. They must supplement their diet with animal prey and other kinds of fruits.

CHANGING IDEAS

Nat's discoveries have altered how people look at quetzals and avocado plants. They have also provided important insights into how mutualistic relationships evolve. Far from being the friendly process that many scientists imagined, it can often resemble a war between species. The bird's objective in this war is simply to get as much food as possible as easily as possible. The plant's objective is to get its seeds dispersed without using up all its energy and nutrients making fruits. The whole battle is a high-wire act and is driven by *natural selection*—the weeding-out process that leads to evolution and the creation of new species. The winners are those plants and birds that, over time, achieve the best balance in their different, competing needs for survival.

Today, Nat is a professor of biology at Bowdoin College in Maine. He spends most of his research time studying the behavior of sparrows in Canada, but he has maintained his interest in the evolution of tropical plants and animals. Each year, he returns to Monteverde to check up on several study sites where he has planted wild avocado trees. Nat hopes that his work will provide further clues about evolution and animal-plant interactions. These clues may help us understand not only quetzals and avocado trees but also the complex processes that have created life itself.

THE BROWN JAY: AVIAN ENEMY OR SOCIAL SUPERSTAR?

Not all of Monteverde's birds are flashy spectacles like the resplendent quetzal or three-wattled bellbird. One of the most common avian residents is a drab, brown-and-white bird called the brown jay.

Brown jays haven't always lived in Monteverde. Originally inhabitants of drier lowland areas, they first showed up in Monteverde in the early 1960s, quickly moving onto the farms and dairy pastures people had created. Their population grew rapidly, and now their raucous cries can be heard in almost every part of the community. Many naturalists view the brown jays with disdain, calling them a "weed species" and associating them with the negative effects of human development. The birds also raise concerns because of their aggressive habits, which include robbing the nests of other birds. Not every scientist, however, views the bird with contempt.

Biologist Marcy Lawton conducted field research on the jays in the 1970s and 1980s. Her work unraveled many of the basic behavior patterns of brown jay life.

Unlike many other birds, brown jays live in social groups, or flocks, of up to 20 birds each. In a flock, only one brood, or group of young, is usually raised each year, but the birds' mating system is complex and often variable. Several females may lay eggs in the same or separate nests, and this can result in multiple broods. One of the fascinating aspects of brown jay behavior is that responsibility for the young birds is shared by the entire group. Besides the mothers and fathers, other group members called helpers defend the group's territory, warn against predators, and even bring food to the mother jay and her young. Marcy and other scientists believe this cooperative care increases the chances that brown jay young will survive.

Dean Williams, a former graduate student of Marcy's, has inherited her interest in brown jays. As a master's student and later as a doctoral student at Purdue University, Dean worked with Marcy to learn even more

Dean Williams uses live traps such as this one to catch and band birds for his long-term studies on brown jays.

about brown jay behavior. One question Dean and Marcy have tried to answer concerns the growing population of the jays around Monteverde. Between 1978 and 1987, the number of birds in Marcy's and Dean's study area increased from 143 to 305. The number of flocks and the average flock size also increased. Dean and Marcy wondered whether the higher population density made the jays behave more aggressively toward each other.

In 1978, Marcy observed only eight aggressive interactions between jays. These included birds chasing each other, forcing other birds from the nest, and stealing food. By 1988 and 1990, however, Dean observed 89 aggressive interactions between jays. Dean and Marcy aren't sure why aggressive interactions increased so much. Aggression was mostly between females trying to breed in the same flock. Because each jay flock usually raises only one brood each year, these interactions may indicate that available habitat in the Monteverde area is filling up. Females can no longer stake out a new territory if they want to leave a flock and build their own nest. As a result, competition for who gets to mate within established flocks is increasing.

Dean, Marcy, and their colleagues are also interested in how family relationships influence behavior within and among groups. To answer such questions, Dean and his assistants have spent hundreds of hours observing different groups of jays. They've also undertaken an extensive live-trapping program. When they catch a bird, they band it with colored leg bands to allow easy identification in the field. They also take blood samples to conduct genetic studies of the birds. Dean and others hope that these studies will allow them to establish parent/chick relationships between birds and better understand the pros and cons of the jays' complex behavior.

Brown jays only moved into the Monteverde area after humans created pastures and other clearings.

Cloud Forest Trouble

One of the things that makes cloud forests so special is that they grow only in small areas on the tops of mountains. Not every mountain in the tropics has a cloud forest on top of it. The cloud forest ecosystem has developed only in certain places where the trade winds, altitude, and weather patterns are just right. While making them special, the rarity of cloud forests also makes them extremely vulnerable to human disturbances.

Threats to the cloud forest come from many sources. Illegal hunting, or poaching, of animals and plants has been a big problem in all tropical forests, including the cloud forest. Poachers exterminated white-tail deer from the Monteverde area before the Preserve was established, and the animals are just now coming back. Ocelots, macaws, and resplendent quetzals have also been killed for sport and food. Plants, such as orchids, are stolen for collectors, and some, including a small species of palm tree, have been collected for the delicious pulp, or palmito, found in the centers of their stalks.

To protect the plants and animals in the cloud forest, a group called the Monteverde Conservation League (see chapter six) hires full-time guards to patrol the Preserve. The presence of the guards makes poachers

Once exterminated from Monteverde by hunters, white-tail deer are now moving back into the area.

think twice before entering the Preserve. It also helps address a second major problem: squatters.

Squatters are people who settle on a piece of land without owning or renting it. Squatting is legal in Costa Rica and has a long history there. Many years ago, squatters helped settle wild, remote parts of the country, much as U.S. pioneers "tamed" the West. In Costa Rica, a squatter would find a piece of land, clear it, and make a living on it. By doing so, the squatter obtained legal rights to the land, even if the land was officially owned by someone else.

Squatting is a reasonable way to settle new territory in a country with a lot of land and low population. It prevents rich and powerful people from buying up and controlling large areas that they don't need and aren't using. The problem in Costa Rica and many other countries is that the human population has exploded. Between 1950 and 1995, Costa Rica's human population increased from 860,000 to almost three and a half million. The consequences of this population growth have been enormous. Although the country has made admirable efforts to protect examples of its natural heritage in parks and preserves, it has suffered the highest rate of deforestation in Central America.

Much of the deforestation has been caused by large timber and agricultural companies. Squatters, however, have posed a significant problem in the country's remaining natural areas. Squatters are often very poor people and are desperate to improve their lives. Because most of the other land in Costa Rica has already been settled, many squatters have moved into parks and preserves and begun carving out small patches of forest to make a living. Until recently, Costa Rica's legal system has been such that if the squatters were not evicted from lands within 30 days, then they earned certain legal rights to stay. After one year, squatters could even claim legal ownership to the property they had "settled."

In February 1996, however, the Costa Rican government passed new regulations governing squatters in forested lands. Under the new legislation, owners of forested lands can register their lands with the government. Registered lands then become protected from squatters, and police are required to remove squatters within five days of their being reported by landowners. This will make protecting the Monteverde Cloud Forest Preserve and other preserves much easier, but it still doesn't completely solve the squatting problem. One major stumbling block for many landowners is that they originally bought land from squatters who had no legal title to the properties. Without a legal title, it is so far impossible for preserve managers to register their forest lands. People in Monteverde and elsewhere in Costa Rica are working hard to resolve this issue, but it will be some time before the cloud forest is legally out of the woods.

A FENCE IS NOT ENOUGH

Not all of the threats to Monteverde occur within the Preserve. Clearing of land outside the Preserve also threatens the animals and plants within. Coffee-growers, dairy farmers, and cattle ranchers have cleared the forest around the southern and western boundaries of Monteverde. These people work hard trying to make a living, but their activities threaten several cloud forest species, including the resplendent quetzal.

Partly because of Nat Wheelwright's findings that quetzals migrate up and down the mountains to find food, scientists became concerned with whether the Monteverde Preserve was large enough to protect the quetzal. To answer the question, two biologists, George Powell and Robin Bjork, decided to investigate where the birds went during the year and what resources they depended on. They attached radio transmitters to 21 quetzals over a period of three years, from 1989 to 1991. The scientists followed the birds with radio tracking equipment to see where they were going.

Coffee plantations have been a major reason for deforestation near Monteverde and elsewhere in Costa Rica.

In Costa Rica and many other countries, forests are cut down to make way for cattle grazing.

George and Robin's results showed that the quetzals were spending significant portions of their time feeding on fruits outside of the Preserve. For part of the year, the birds fed primarily down on the Pacific side of the mountains below the Preserve. During other parts of the year, they foraged on the Atlantic side, also outside of the Preserve.

This was a huge concern to the Preserve's managers because it meant that the quetzal was vulnerable to being wiped out by influences over which they had no control. To keep this from happening, the Preserve managers decided to purchase 2,300 hectares (5,750 acres) of additional forest on the Atlantic side of the Preserve. This would protect crucial feeding grounds that the quetzals depended on for at least part of the year. They also began working with farmers and ranchers on the Pacific side of the Preserve to help them protect the remaining trees that the quetzals visited (see chapter six). These efforts may help ensure the survival of quetzals far into the future. Unfortunately, these kinds of activities aren't enough to protect some of the cloud forest's other treasures. (see Field Notes: "Bonking Across Borders").

BONKING ACROSS BORDERS

The expansion of the Monteverde Preserve to include enough habitat for the resplendent quetzal has proved to be a major challenge for Preserve managers. But this is nothing compared to the problems presented by Monteverde's other famous bird migrant, the three-wattled bellbird.

After their work tracking the quetzal, George Powell and Robin Bjork turned their attention to the bellbird. From 1991 through 1994, George and Robin radio-tagged 48 bellbirds in Monteverde. Their goal was to find out where the birds went during the year and whether adequate protection was being given to the birds' habitats.

The two scientists found that the bellbirds traveled to at least four different locations during any given year. After breeding on Monteverde's Atlantic slope from March through June, the birds crossed the continental divide to forests on the Pacific side of the mountains. (Some of the birds also breed on the Pacific side of the continental divide, in and around Monteverde.) Between September and

November, the bellbirds again crossed the divide and flew hundreds of kilometers away to lowland rain forests in southeastern Nicaragua and northeastern Costa Rica. Finally, in November and December, the birds flew all the way back across Costa Rica to lowland rain forests on the country's Pacific side.

George and Robin's work clearly showed that no single preserve could hope to protect all the habitat that the bellbirds need to survive. Their data also demonstrated how vulnerable migratory species are to habitat destruction. If just one of the bellbirds' four habitats disappears, it could easily wipe out the entire bellbird population. Unfortunately, this has come very close to happening. Although three of the birds' four habitats are large enough to ensure the birds' survival in the near future, the fourth—the mountain forests on the Pacific side of the Preserve—has been almost totally destroyed by human activities. Only about 1,870 hectares (4,620 acres) of this forest remain, and much of this is in poor condition.

From their study, George and Robin concluded that the bellbird faces a major population decline if immediate steps are not taken to protect more of its habitat. Perhaps more important, their work shows that we can't just set aside a small area and hope to protect all of the animals and plants living there. Instead, we must study the biology of animals and plants and create systems of preserves that account for all of their needs. As in the case of bellbirds, creating such preserves will require national and international cooperation. Only by doing this can we ensure the survival of species long into the future.

MOUNTAIN GOLD

In May 1963, Monteverde resident Jerry James led two visiting biologists, Jay Savage and Norman Scott, to a patch of forest on the continental divide, not far from where Bob Lawton's study site lies today. The hike was difficult and very wet, but Savage and Scott had reason to be excited. After all, this was no ordinary outing. Today, James was leading them to a spectacular new species.

The trio walked for more than an hour, sliding down steep, muddy trails and stumbling over tree roots jutting out of the ground. Then, they came upon an incredible sight. Hopping in and around several shallow pools were hundreds of bright orange toads. Many male toads were locked together with females in *amplexus*, or mating position. Other males searched aggressively for females, even trying to dislodge rival males from the backs of females they were mating with. Savage was amazed by the new creatures, which were totally unknown to biologists. In a scientific paper in which he first described the toads, Savage wrote:

> The first individuals collected were a small series of males, all uniform bright orange in color. I must confess that my initial response when I saw them was one of disbelief and suspicion that someone had dipped the examples in enamel paint. The females proved to be equally astonishing, for they are olive to black with a series of large spots of brightest scarlet and without any hint of orange in their coloration. The new form is assuredly the most spectacularly colored *Bufo* [toad] known and is among the gaudiest of anurans [toads and frogs].

Savage decided to name the toad *Bufo periglenes*. *Bufo* is the genus of amphibians that includes all toads; *periglenes* is a Greek word that means "very bright." Other people dubbed the new species the golden toad.

Since its discovery, the golden toad has intrigued herpetologists—scientists who study amphibians and reptiles—and other naturalists the world over. Its striking color, the fact that males and females are different colors, and its extremely limited distribution all set it apart from other toad species. Scientists scoured the Monteverde area and found only half a dozen breeding sites for the toad. All of these sites were located in the Brillante area of the Preserve, between 1,480 and 1,600 meters (4,850 and 5,250 feet) above sea level. What's more, the golden toad population was small, numbering no more than several thousand. For most of the year, this small population stayed hidden underground. Each April or May, however, the toads emerged for a few short weeks to engage in their mating frenzy.

During the next 20 years, a number of scientists conducted research projects on the toad's biology and behavior. From these studies, scientists learned about basic aspects of the toad's physiology and reproduction. Then, in 1988, biologist Martha, or Marty, Crump from the University of Florida was awarded a two-year National Geographic grant to study the toad's breeding habits.

Marty had already spent many hours during the 1987 rainy season huddled inside her raincoat, watching the toads mate and lay their eggs in their remote mountain home. Rain fell almost unceasingly during that time, creating wet, cold, muddy working conditions. "It was really quite miserable," Marty recalls. With the heart of a true biologist, however, she persisted and was all set to begin her more extensive two-year study the following year. But in 1988, Marty ran into an unexpected problem.

The golden toad disappeared.

NOT-SO-STORMY WEATHER

The golden toad wasn't the only amphibian to perform a disappearing act in 1988. During the same period, 20 of 50 frog and toad species disappeared from

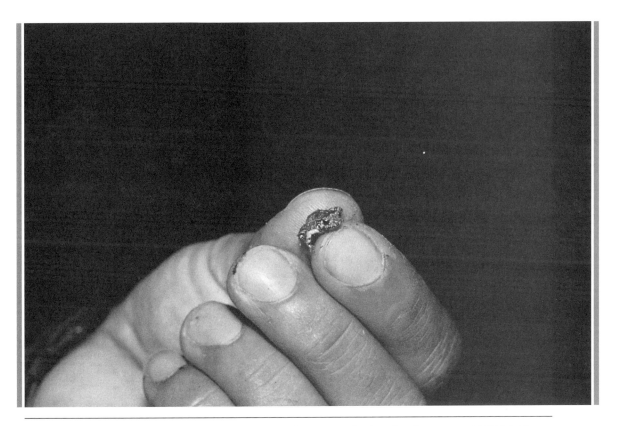

Twenty of Monteverde's 50 amphibian species disappeared after the disastrous 1987 El Niño.

a 30-square-kilometer (11.5-square-mile) area of Monteverde. One notable species was the harlequin frog, a stunning black-and-yellow creature with a bright red belly. The harlequin frog was usually very common along streams and rivers near Monteverde, but like the golden toad, it totally vanished from the area after 1987. Populations of glass frogs and members of the genus *Eleutherodactylus* also crashed.

After the golden toads disappeared, Marty Crump began searching for an explanation. At first she believed that the years following 1987 simply hadn't offered the right conditions for the toads to breed. Other species of frogs and toads are known to stay dormant or hidden, sometimes for years, until breeding conditions are right. Because the golden toads stayed underground most of the year anyway, Marty reasoned that they were just waiting until conditions improved. As the golden toads failed to appear in 1989, 1990, and the following years, however, this explanation began to look doubtful.

An alternative explanation came from one of Marty's former graduate students, Alan Pounds. Alan had first visited Monteverde as Marty's field assistant in 1981. He returned in 1982 to conduct his Ph.D. research on harlequin frogs. He put in many days studying the frogs but was foiled by a strange weather pattern known as *El Niño*, which caused the frogs to behave abnormally. Instead of working on the frogs, Alan switched to studying a group of lizards called anoles. After his Ph.D. work, he returned to Florida for two years and then came back to Monteverde on a post-doctoral position with the Organization for Tropical Studies. He ended up staying on in Monteverde, working for the Preserve and eventually becoming its Research Director.

Alan was familiar with the history of the golden toad. Through his work in the Preserve, he was also aware of the declines of the many other amphibian species following 1987. Alan, though, wasn't convinced that the weather in 1988 had been bad enough to prevent the golden toads and other amphibians from breeding. Instead, he decided to look more closely at the weather *in* 1987, the last year the toads had appeared.

Like the years 1982 and 1983, 1987 was an *El Niño* year. During *El Niños*, abnormally warm ocean temperatures cause worldwide shifts in weather patterns. Places that are normally dry often receive large amounts of rain. Places that are usually wet may experience extreme droughts.

When Marty Crump had originally looked at the weather of 1987, she had concluded that it was wet enough to allow golden toads to breed. What she didn't take into account was that an unusually wet spring storm had hit Monteverde in April while she was observing the toads. From this, she had assumed that the rest of 1987 had also been wet.

Alan Pounds, though, began looking at the other months of 1987. He decided to re-analyze the events of that year and contacted Marty Crump to see if she'd share her data on the harlequin frog with him. Working together, they came up with a different conclusion than Marty had reached on her own. Far from being a very wet year, they discovered that 1987 as a whole had been much drier and much warmer than usual. They concluded that these extreme conditions had probably affected the golden toad and other amphibian populations, but how?

DEADLY POSSIBILITIES

Neither Alan nor Marty thought that the warm, dry weather by itself could totally wipe out the golden toads. They hypothesized that the unusual conditions were accompanied by some other event that harmed the toads. What that other event might have been, remained unclear. High levels of ultraviolet radiation (UV) from the sun were one possibility. The problem with that option was that the toads spent most of their time underground and even when they were active, they were protected by a thick canopy of trees.

Another possibility was that a pulse of acid rain had hit Monteverde during 1987. Because of their moist absorbing skins, frogs, toads, and other amphibians are especially susceptible to acid rain and often die from it. However, measurements of rain and fog in 1988 and later years revealed no abnormal acidity reaching Monteverde, so the possibility that it had done so in 1987 seemed unlikely.

A third possibility was that the toads were weakened by the dry, warm

Fertilizers and pesticides used on lowland crops can be carried into the atmosphere and end up in the cloud forest, many miles away.

conditions of 1987 and had been hit by a virus or other disease that wiped out the adult animals. Alan now favors this hypothesis, because of recent work in Australia indicating that viruses are killing frogs in that country. Like Monteverde, Australia has experienced many climate fluctuations and spells of dry, warm weather. Scientists worldwide now attribute these extreme weather patterns to the Greenhouse Effect, an increase in world temperatures caused by pollution in the atmosphere. Alan thinks it likely that the physical stress created by the drier weather may have caused Monteverde's amphibians to suffer from diseases similar to those affecting Australian amphibians.

One final possibility was that some kind of pollution had killed the toads. "When I started getting interested in this," Alan explains, "I started talking to environmental chemists and toxicologists and bouncing ideas off of them. I started getting pretty frightened just by the possibilities, the way things could work."

In the lowlands of Costa Rica, for instance, farmers apply large quantities of fertilizers and toxic pesticides to their crops. Many of these are carried into the air and washed out of the sky by rain and fog. Measurements in Monteverde during March and April have shown that

FROGS UNDER GLASS

Like many other scientists who have come to Monteverde, Alan Pounds has developed interests beyond pure scientific research. "My inclination," he explains, "has shifted more toward applied conservation mixed with research. For example, raising and doing experimental releases of frogs into the wild will perhaps yield valuable scientific information on why animals are declining."

Such experimental releases are not without controversy. Some scientists object to releasing captive-bred animals into the wild because they may contaminate the species' gene pools and disrupt natural ecological processes. Captive-bred animals may also introduce diseases or parasites into wild populations. Alan, though, believes that such releases have a lot to contribute. "Most discussions of release programs," he says, "ignore the scientific value of it. If releases are done within an experimental design, they can help you answer some questions about conservation or about basic natural history of the animals that affects their survival."

In order to pursue his interests, Alan has been constructing the Golden Toad Research Center on his land next to the Monteverde Preserve. The heart of the observatory is a giant greenhouse 12 meters long by 10 meters wide (about 39 by 32 feet). Inside, he has designed a large pool with a flowing stream and even a rain chamber that simulates natural precipitation. When completed, the observatory will also include a laboratory, living quarters for researchers, and several outdoor ponds.

His goal is to make the observatory a center for studying amphibians in both field and laboratory conditions. In the greenhouse and outdoor ponds, he plans to raise many species of frogs and some reptiles, especially those that have declined at Monteverde but exist in larger populations elsewhere. He hopes to learn more about the animals' biology so that people can make better decisions about protecting them. Eventually, he may also release captive-bred frogs back into places where they have disappeared.

Besides serving as a conservation tool, the Golden Toad Research Center may help educate visitors to Monteverde. Alan is considering opening the center to the public, both to teach people about amphibians and to help finance amphibian research activities. This, in turn, will help support conservation efforts and attract important tourist dollars to the Monteverde community.

high levels of nitrates and phosphates are carried into the cloud forest from the lowlands, where many fields are burned after harvesting. Alan and Marty concluded that a pulse of this type of pollution could have affected the golden toads and other amphibian species.

WORLDWIDE TRAGEDIES

Whatever its cause, the disappearance of amphibians from Monteverde was not an isolated incident. Amphibians of many species have been disappearing around the globe during the past 20 years. The causes of these declines are probably different in each case, but they have long-term consequences for our planet. Amphibians are an important resource for humans. They eat harmful insects and provide food for other species. Some, like the poison-arrow frogs of Central and South America, are the source of important chemicals that may be used to treat cancer and other diseases.

Frogs, toads, and salamanders are also a great source of joy to people. Many people raise and care for these animals. Many more delight in observing them in the wild. Before it disappeared, the golden toad was, like the quetzal, an important reason why people visited Monteverde. Its probable extinction not only leaves us poorer spiritually, but it also means the loss of thousands of tourist dollars for the people living in the area.

Since the toad's disappearance, some of the other amphibian populations that crashed have begun to rebound. The *Eleutherodactylus* frogs, for instance, were rare for several years, but have become fairly abundant again. This is good news for frog-eating snakes and other animals, many of which also declined in numbers after the frogs disappeared.

Unfortunately, the golden toads and harlequin frogs have failed to reappear. For the harlequin frog, the disaster is not quite complete. They continue to survive in several other places in Costa Rica. Not so with the golden toad; its only known range was the mountains of Monteverde.

In an effort to find the toads, Alan Pounds and other scientists have been conducting regular surveys of the toads' former breeding sites since 1987. In 1988 and 1989, a few solitary golden toads were found near their old haunts. Between 1990 and 1996, however, researchers failed to find a single golden toad. Some scientists hold out hope that the toads are still in hiding and will one day reappear. With each passing year, however, the chances for such a miracle grow less. Marty, Alan, and other biologists now accept that the golden toad is probably gone for good, an irreplaceable casualty in the human conquest of Planet Earth.

In order to conduct experiments on Umbonia *fitness, Karen Masters raises the treehoppers on their host plants in a nursery near Monteverde.*

Unlike most other animals the treehopper Umbonia *actually seems to benefit from inbreeding.*

Blue-crowned motmots are commonly seen perched around Monteverde. The birds hunt insects, lizards, and other small prey.

Male ithomiine, or clearwing, butterflies pass both sperm and protective chemicals to females during mating.

The male resplendent quetzal is
Monteverde's most popular
attraction. The birds only nest
in high-altitude tropical forests,
where they find an abundance of
wild avocado fruits to feed on.

Male three-wattled bellbirds emit loud metallic bonks to attract females with which to mate. Studies by George Powell and Robin Bjork showed that during the year, bellbirds travel between forests hundreds of kilometers apart.

Before they disappeared in 1988, hundreds of golden toads emerged from their hiding places each rainy season to engage in mating "frenzies."

Locked in amplexus, the male fertilizes strings of golden toad eggs as the female releases them.

Like the golden toad, the harlequin frog disappeared from Monteverde after 1987.

Dean Williams often has to scramble over rough terrain to count and observe his and Marcy Lawton's brown jay flocks.

Most of the forest around Monteverde's Pacific slope has been cleared for cow pastures and farms.

The spectacular Peñas Blancas Valley on the Atlantic side of the continental divide was purchased and incorporated into the Preserve with the help of private donations from around the world.

An *abundance of water has helped create the unique cloud forest ecosystem. Protecting this water source is essential for the survival of both the forest and the people living nearby.*

Chapter Six

Cloud Forest Conservation

Monteverde is not the only montane forest threatened by human activities. In Ecuador, Venezuela, Hawaii, Papua New Guinea, Africa, and many other places, these forests are beset by a host of problems, including logging, poaching, oil exploration, and settlement by the desperate poor. Despite the loss of the golden toad and other setbacks, however, Monteverde offers an example of what can be done to protect these unique ecosystems and the many benefits they provide.

As this book's introduction explained, conservation at Monteverde began with the first Quakers, or Friends, who settled there in 1951. These industrious people bought 1,500 hectares (3,750 acres) of mountainous forest and began to establish farms. However, 630 hectares (1,570 acres) of the property—from the present-day visitor center up to the continental divide—was still virgin forest. The Quakers realized that this forest protected essential water supplies that they needed to survive, so they decided to set aside this forest for watershed.

For 20 years, the Friends built up their community and their farms. Meanwhile, they continued to protect the 630 hectares they had set aside for watershed. Every once in a while, they would have to remove some squatters from the property, but few serious problems arose. The Friends could see, however, that as the population of Costa Rica grew, the pressures on their forest and surrounding forest areas would increase. At the same time, biologists began to recognize the importance of the cloud forest not only for watershed, but for the diverse collection of plants and animals, or "biological diversity," living there.

A NATURAL TREASURE

George Powell was the first biologist to do extensive field work in Monteverde. In 1970, he began studying the behavior of mixed feeding flocks of birds (see chapter four) on the land of John and Doris Campbell, two of Monteverde's original settlers. John and Doris had a particular interest in conservation and had left as much of their land as possible in its natural condition. The couple had also kept detailed records of Monteverde's weather over many years —a service that proved invaluable to biologists who would later work there. As George Powell got to know the cloud forest, he grew to appreciate its uniqueness and became increasingly concerned with protecting it.

George convinced a group called the Tropical Science Center in San José, Costa Rica, to take an active role in administering and expanding the original piece of cloud forest that the Quakers had protected. The Friends welcomed this because it would reduce their own responsibilities and provide scientific management of the property. They leased their whole 630 hectares to the Tropical Science Center for one colon per year—about three cents. This, in turn, led to the formal creation of the Monteverde Cloud Forest Preserve.

With contributions from The Nature Conservancy, the World Wildlife Fund, the RARE Center for Tropical Research, and many Audubon Society chapters, the Tropical Science Center coordinated the purchase of additional forest lands to expand and protect the Preserve. By the end of the 1980s, the

Center had acquired about 4,000 additional hectares (10,000 acres), most of it virgin forest up on the divide and on the wetter Atlantic slope of the mountain range.

About that time, however, Monteverde residents and scientists also became concerned about the forest on the drier Pacific slope of the range. Because of a steady influx of settlers to the area, very little of this drier forest remained. In 1982, 14 people got together to form the Monteverde Conservation League (MCL). The MCL began a campaign to expand the Preserve's holdings and purchased about 2,000 more hectares (5,000 acres), which the Tropical Science Center agreed to incorporate into the 4,000 hectares that they had already protected. But that wasn't the end of land protection in Monteverde.

THE POWER OF YOUTH

In 1987, MCL member Sharon Kinsman gave a talk to a group of fifth- and sixth-grade school children in Sweden. She described Monteverde and the conservation work being done there. The students became excited about the cloud forest and its protection. They decided they would like to help out and began raising money. They sent a check to the Monteverde Conservation League, and the MCL bought some land with it, naming the new acquisition the Swedish Children's Rain Forest.

No one in Monteverde could have ever predicted what happened next.

Throughout Sweden, children began raising money for rain forest protection. In all, they sent the MCL more than a million dollars. News of their efforts spread to other countries. In the United Kingdom, the United States, Canada, Germany, Japan, and the Netherlands, children organized to raise money to protect the cloud forest.

SCHOOL IN THE CLOUDS

In 1990, Meg LaVal and three or four friends were having lunch and discussing education in the Monteverde area. They calculated that a large number of young children would be entering school in the next few years. Instead of simply enlarging the present schools in the area, they

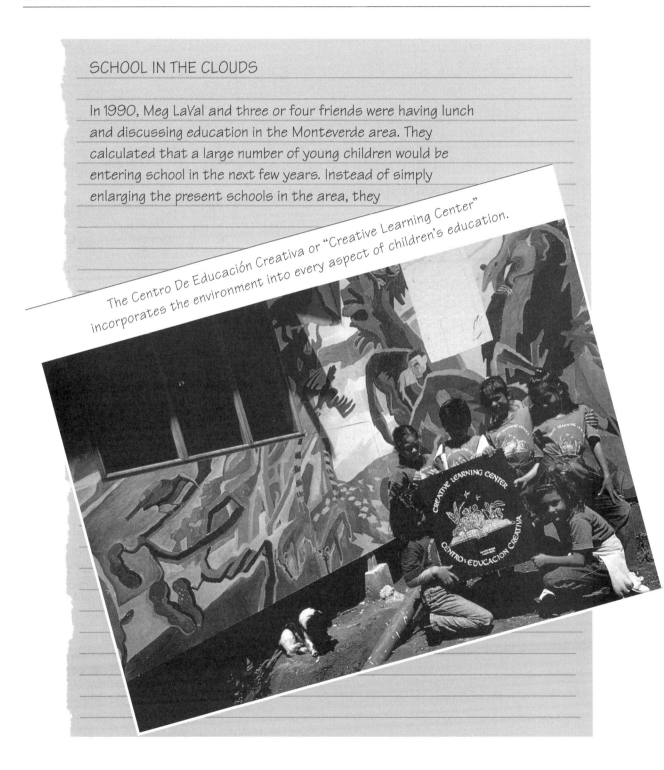

The Centro De Educación Creativa or "Creative Learning Center" incorporates the environment into every aspect of children's education.

thought it would be great to create a new school that stressed environmental education.

Together with Meg's husband Richard and other community members, they opened the Centro De Educación Creativa (Creative Learning Center) school in 1990. They began with kindergarten and have been adding one grade each year as the oldest kids become ready to move up. With the help of volunteer Dr. Sybil Terres Gilmar, they put together a child-centered curriculum that emphasized environmental education. "We figured everything is interrelated," Richard LaVal explains. "So we work the environment into math and biology and history and every other subject. Now, we have a curriculum that incorporates all that."

How do the kids like it?

"They love it," Richard replies. "Every day they're outside. We have a 42-hectare (104-acre) campus that is mostly forest, and it stretches all the way up to the continental divide."

Besides creating a positive learning environment, the school offers students practical benefits. "Because it's a bilingual school," says Richard, "classes are taught in both Spanish and English. When they graduate, children will be prepared to work in the tourist industry here and in many other jobs. That's one reason our school is so popular."

The CEC school is one of the few schools of its kind in the world, but with luck, it won't be the last. As our environmental problems worsen, the need to understand the environment will become increasingly important. Schools with a strong commitment to environmental education will undoubtedly play an important role in teaching all of us to respect and understand our fragile environmental resources.

With the money that the children sent, the MCL purchased more than 16,000 hectares (40,000 acres) of forest land in and around Monteverde. They called this new Preserve the International Children's Rain Forest, and it has become one of the largest privately owned tropical forest preserves in the world. To keep squatters and poachers out of the preserve, the MCL hires full-time guards to patrol the forest. The MCL also works to educate local people about the importance of protecting forest lands and their plants and animals.

CONSERVATION FOR EVERYONE

Unfortunately, buying and patrolling land does not ensure protection of the cloud forest's many plant and animal species. The resplendent quetzal is a good example of this. As chapter five explained, the quetzal often uses trees on farms and ranches outside of the Preserve. If the people who own these farms decide to cut down their trees, it could quickly spell disaster for the quetzal.

Carlos Guindon has worked with George Powell, the MCL, and other scientists to address this issue. Carlos comes from a family of dedicated conservationists. His father, Wolf Guindon, was one of the original Quaker settlers in Monteverde. Over the years, he has become an expert on Monteverde's plants and animals. In fact, it would be hard to find a scientist in Monteverde who has not depended on Wolf's knowledge when conducting research on the cloud forest.

Carlos' brothers have also been active in conservation work. Benito, Tomás, and Ricardo have often assisted scientists in their research and have served as guides for tourists visiting the Preserve. Carlos, though, has earned a special distinction. He is the first person born and raised in Monteverde who has gone on to earn his Ph.D. in biology. His goal is to help protect Monteverde's biological diversity and unique forest habitats through research, education, and community involvement.

To learn more about how to do this, Carlos Guindon has been studying how the quetzal, the three-wattled bellbird, and other large fruit-eating bird species use resources outside the protected Preserve. What he has discovered is that bird species differ in their abilities to reach patches of forest that are not connected to the main Monteverde Preserve. Bellbirds, for instance, will cross

long distances over farmland to reach a patch of forest with fruiting trees (see chapter five, Field Notes: "Bonking Across Borders"). Quetzals and other birds, however, are much less inclined or able to do so.

Using his data and the radio-tracking work of George Powell and Robin Bjork, Carlos and others have begun an ambitious project to integrate farmers and farms into a regional conservation management plan. First, they identi-

Ricardo Guindon, brother of Carlos Guindon, helps educate tourists by leading nighttime walks through the Preserve.

Many farmers around Monteverde have begun planting wind breaks. The wind breaks not only help protect fields but also produce wood for farmers and food for wildlife.

fied the areas that quetzals and other birds depend on the most. Then, they proposed to create a series of *microcorridors* that would connect these key areas with the main Preserve. "The idea," says Carlos, "is to increase landowner

In efforts to increase quetzal numbers, biologists have set up more than 30 "quetzal boxes" around Monteverde. Good nesting trees for the quetzals may be in short supply, but the boxes may help rectify that situation.

awareness of the importance of connecting forest fragments together for wildlife."

Creating the microcorridors is not an easy task. It involves protecting patches of forest that still exist and establishing new forests in fields and pastures where trees have been removed. Working with the MCL and using money from the RARE Center for Tropical Research, the National Fish and Wildlife Foundation, and the Hardin Generativity Trust, Carlos and George Powell have helped farmers identify patches of forest on their farms that are valuable to quetzals and other birds. They have also helped provide money and technical assistance to farmers so that they can fence their forests and prevent cattle from trampling young trees and other forest plants.

In the effort to reforest fields and pastures, Carlos's team has provided additional assistance with fencing and tree-planting. Reforestation is not an entirely new concept for many of the area's farmers. Many were already involved in reforestation efforts promoted by the MCL. Since 1988, the MCL (with funding from World Wildlife Canada and the Canadian International Development Agency) has assisted farmers in planting half a million trees around Monteverde, most of them in the form of windbreaks. The MCL maintains two nurseries that grow more than 40 different kinds of trees, most of them native species that quetzals and other birds can use. Their reforestation efforts offer advantages to both wildlife and farmers. By blocking the wind, the trees keep pastures from drying out quickly. Many of the trees also add nitrogen to the soil, reducing the needs for chemical fertilizers. An added bonus is that the trees supply the farmers with wood for fence posts, fuel, and lumber.

"A lot of the farmers now have been involved in planting windbreaks," says Carlos. "So they realize how difficult and costly it is to establish trees on the farm." With this realization, many farmers see the value in protecting the patches of forests they have left. Carlos and his co-workers are also continuing to work on increasing farmer awareness through a process called *agricultural extension*, or farmer outreach sensitization. It is part of a seven-year program envisioned by Carlos and George to improve Costa Rica's biological diversity by involving local landowners in conservation. But the biologists don't do all the teaching. Farmers also have a lot of knowledge to share with scientists.

"It's a two-way process," says Carlos. "The idea is to take information from farmers, use that information, and turn it around when it comes to extension. So the landowner knowledge of what's in their forests—and what they use and value—is incorporated into our efforts. That way, when you're reforesting, you are using species that the landowners recognize as being important. This is more effective than just planting species of biological value."

VALUING HUMAN BEINGS

The microcorridor project and reforestation efforts are not the only programs that seek to involve local people and improve their lives. In 1986, residents of Monteverde established a nonprofit group called the Monteverde Institute (MVI). As their Statement of Mission explains, the institute is:

> a non-profit educational association dedicated to peace, justice and knowledge. It provides and coordinates programs that promote the appreciation of diversity and communality, spirituality, and the well-being of living things. These educational opportunities are designed for students from abroad and Costa Rica, and for residents of the Monteverde community and surrounding areas.

One of the MVI's main activities is to coordinate courses in tropical forest ecology for the University of California Education Abroad Program, the Council on International Educational Exchange, and the Evergreen State College in Olympia, Washington. These courses are ten weeks long and teach stu-

SHARING IMAGES OF NATURE

"We are research biologists," explain Patricia and Michael Fogden. "But we decided early on that we didn't want to be confined to a narrow niche, which is what happens if you keep going in the sciences. So we moved to Monteverde as our base 15 years ago and gave ourselves five years to make it work. Fortunately, it did."

Patricia and Michael Fogden have indeed made it work. As photographers, they have captured some of the most stunning views of nature ever recorded, including golden toads, quetzals, eyelash vipers, and countless other subjects. Their specialty is the tropics, and they travel widely in their work.

"We pick topics that have a particular focus," Michael explains. "We can't just go to a place and shoot whatever we see. I mean, that's fine, but the problem is that then you have stock agency shots such as landscapes. Instead, we usually have a number of animals we need to shoot. We don't necessarily need to get every one on our list, but we need about 70 percent of them."

Is the work dangerous? To an outside observer, it may seem so. Michael has contracted the disease leishmaniasis twice while

Biologists-turned-photographers Michael Fogden and Patricia Fogden have captured some of the most stunning images of the natural world ever recorded.

working. The photography team has also spent time in politically unstable areas, such as Namibia during that country's war for independence. Still, Patricia and Michael feel most threatened not in developing countries or the wilderness, but when visiting crime-ridden cities of the United States.

The team's biggest challenge is not avoiding danger but getting the right shots. For example, to photograph birds called sunbitterns in the Peñas Blancas Valley below Monteverde, the Fogdens sat in a blind for six to eight hours a day. They watched and photographed the birds from the time the eggs hatched out until they fledged. "It turned out to be a useful study, too," Michael says, "because we recorded most of the prey items fed to the chicks, something no one had ever done with sunbitterns before. And that's something we try to do with our work—accomplish some useful research as well as photography."

How can they be so patient?

"Michael is a fanatic," Patricia says.

"Yes," Michael admits. "I guess it's more like being possessed than patient. I am extremely single-minded, sometimes to the point of diminishing returns. But if we weren't like that, a lot of times we wouldn't get the shots. And we usually do get them."

During the last 15 years, the Fogdens' photographs have been published in hundreds of magazines and books (including this one. See the second color insert). They have also written articles about the animals and plants they photograph. Their work has delighted people around the world and has also contributed to conservation efforts. By sharing their images and knowledge with others, they help educate people about the beauty and uniqueness of tropical species. This, in turn, inspires people to care about protecting tropical forests and the other remarkable ecosystems of our planet.

dents not only about biology but also about Costa Rican culture and such topics as agro-ecology, traditional farming practices, ecotourism, and Spanish. The MVI also coordinates shorter courses for high school and college students, teachers, and other adults seeking briefer introductions to the cloud forest and community. Through the Volunteer Center, which is run jointly with the Monteverde Conservation League, the MVI also arranges for volunteer workers to stay with local families. This allows volunteers to hone their Spanish and exchange cultural experience with native Costa Ricans.

The Monteverde Institute has been especially active in working with women of the community. Conservation workers around the world have come to recognize that women are often left out of decision-making even though they are the ones doing much—if not most—of the work supporting families. This imbalance has led to dire social and environmental consequences, because men often make decisions that fail to consider long-range impacts on the environment and their families.

To empower women and give them a greater role in shaping their families' futures, the MVI has conducted women's workshops on self-esteem, leadership, basic nutrition, interpersonal relationships, and other issues that are often overlooked in rural areas. These efforts have paid off. In and around Monteverde, dozens of women have pooled their efforts and resources to form cooperatives. In one of these, La Campesinita, women produce and package fruit cocktail, guava jam, and other delicacies to help support their families and provide a work alternative to more traditional jobs, such as working as maids. Because the women are usually expected to continue their household chores, they take turns caring for each other's children and in this way have bettered themselves and their families.

In another cooperative, Cooperativa Artesanal Santa Elena-Monteverde (CASEM), women produce crafts and other products to sell to tourists and

CASEM *offers the opportunity for men and women to improve their economic condition by selling crafts that they produce at home.*

other visitors to Monteverde. CASEM allows more than 150 women and men to work at home and sell their wares in the CASEM store in the village of Monteverde. CASEM has helped women learn new skills, bring in cash for their families, and communicate with each other. By improving their economic conditions, these people reduce the pressure on the cloud forest to provide them with a living. Also, women often have a closer connection to the environment than their husbands. By having a greater say over their own lives,

The Monteverde community offers an example of how we can all survive while protecting our natural heritage.

they are able to exert greater influence over their families, friends, and neighbors to respect and protect the forests around them.

A REAL PLACE

Monteverde is not perfect. It is a community of real people confronting real problems faced by themselves, the economy, and the environment. Despite the dedication of the members of the community and the scientists who work there, they don't always agree how to do things or achieve as much as they want. Sometimes, forest lands are destroyed or taken over before they can be protected. In other instances, such as the disappearance of the golden toad, people's efforts are defeated by events beyond their control.

Monteverde's greatest strength, however, may not lie in its successes and defeats. It may be in its role as a model for how to approach conservation and sustainable development around the world. As our planet's human population explodes, the pressure to use forests and other natural ecosystems has never been greater. This is as true in Costa Rica as it is in the United States, Asia, and Africa. The question is, "Can we meet the needs of people and still protect at least some of our natural areas?"

The question has no easy answers. The efforts of people in Monteverde, however, demonstrate that by taking a variety of approaches, from scientific research to agricultural and social outreach, we at least have a fighting chance to save some of the natural places that make Earth such an extraordinary place to live. Even more, these efforts help show us that by working together, we have a chance to save ourselves.

Learning More about Tropical Cloud Forests

Although hundreds of books have been written about tropical rain forests in the past ten years, almost none have been written specifically about tropical montane, or cloud, forests. One exception is the recent book by Nalini Nadkarni and Nathaniel Wheelwright, *The Ecology and Conservation of Monteverde* (New York: Oxford University Press, 1997). This book includes chapters by many different scientists. It is written as a reference book but will make fascinating reading for anyone interested in tropical forests. Along the same lines, Daniel Janzen's *Costa Rica Natural History* (Chicago: University of Chicago Press, 1983) provides solid, interesting information about Costa Rica's fabulous biodiversity.

A number of other titles explore topics covered in this book. Mark Moffett's *The High Frontier: Exploring the Tropical Rainforest Canopy* (Cambridge: Harvard University Press, 1993) shares biologists' experiences working in the treetops. Kathryn Phillips's *Tracking the Vanishing Frogs: An Ecological Mystery* (New York: St. Martin's, 1994) is a readable account of the worldwide decline in amphibian populations. E. O. Wilson's *The Diversity of Life* (Cambridge: Harvard University Press, 1992) provides an excellent summary of biodiversity and its importance to human beings. Jonathan Weiner's *The Beak of the Finch* (New York: Knopf, 1994) provides a riveting and entertaining introduction to evolution and Charles Darwin.

One of my favorite general books about tropical rainforests is *Tropical Nature* (New York: Scribners, 1984) by Adrian Forsyth and Ken Miyata. It expresses the wonder of these ecosystems with a great deal of insight and humor. *Portraits of the Rainforest* (Columbia, SC: Camden House, 1996), also by Adrian Forsyth, features stunning photographs by Michael and Patricia Fogden. For general rainforest references, look at *The Last Rain Forests: A World Conservation Atlas* (New York: Oxford University Press, 1990), edited by Mark Collins, and Kathlyn Gay's *Rainforests of the World: a Reference Handbook* (Santa Barbara, CA: ABC-CLIO, 1993). Three general rainforest titles for young adults are James D. Nations's *Tropical Rainforests: Endangered Environment* (New York: Franklin Watts, 1988); *Rainforests* (San Diego: Lucent Books, 1990), by Lois Warburton; and *Earth's Vanishing Forests* (New York: Macmillan, 1991) by Roy A. Gallant.

Finally, for practical information on how to protect tropical biodiversity, check out Scott Lewis's *The rainforest book: how you can save the world's rainforests* (Washington, D.C.: Living Planet, 1990) and *50 Simple Things You Can Do to Save the Earth* (Berkeley, CA: Earth Works, 1989).

Saving Tropical Forests

If you would like to donate money or learn more about how you can protect the cloud forest, contact:

The Children's Rain Forest
c/o The Nature Conservancy, Latin America and Caribbean Division
1815 N. Lynn Street
Arlington, VA 22209
(703) 841-4860

In addition to accepting donations to protect the cloud forest, The Nature Conservancy also runs an "Adopt-an-Acre" program that helps protect tropical forests throughout the world and accepts regular contributions.

Also active in protecting tropical forests is the Rainforest Action Network (RAN). RAN accepts donations and is particularly active in protecting rainforest peoples and stopping destruction of forests by logging, mining, and other activities. RAN may be reached at:

Rainforest Action Network
450 Sansome Street, #700
San Francisco, CA 94111
(415) 398-4404

¡Muchas Gracias!

This book could never have been completed without generous donations of time and energy from dozens of people. First and foremost I'd like to thank Nalini Nadkarni, who introduced me to Monteverde and provided me with countless hours of assistance in planning my visits, obtaining references, and reviewing the manuscript for this book. A special thanks to Bob Law and Susie Newswanger for providing me with a place to stay, hot meals, and a wealth of information while I visited Monteverde. I am grateful to Russell Primm at Grolier for giving this project a home and my editor Scott Prentzas for helping to make this the best book possible. I am also indebted to:

Margaret Adelman, Monteverde
John and Doris Campbell, Monteverde
Francisco Chamberlin, The Monteverde Cloud Forest Preserve
Martha Crump, Northern Arizona University
James Daniels, The University of North Dakota
Vicente Bison Espinoza, Monteverde and the RARE Center for Tropical
    Conservation
Michael and Patricia Fogden, Monteverde
Carlos Guindon, Monteverde and Yale University
Wolf Guindon, Monteverde
William Haber, Monteverde and the Missouri Botanical Garden
Laurie Hunter, The RARE Center for Tropical Conservation
Frank Joyce, The Monteverde Conservation League and the University of
    California Education Abroad Program

Richard and Meg LaVal, Monteverde

Robert Law, The Monteverde Conservation League and Bosque Eterno

Robert Lawton, The University of Alabama in Huntsville

Jack Longino, The Evergreen State College

Alan Masters, Monteverde and the Council on International Educational Exchange

Karen Masters, Monteverde and Princeton University

Martha Moss, Monteverde

Susie Newswanger, Monteverde

Alan J. Pounds, The Monteverde Cloud Forest Preserve and the University of Miami

Gabriel Barboza, Monteverde

Laurie Sanders

Nat Scrimshaw, Sandwich Range Conservation Association, Camden, New Hampshire, and the Monteverde Institute

Ree Sheck, The Monteverde Conservation League

Jenny Rowe, The Community School of South Tamworth, South Tamworth, New Hampshire

Robert Timm, The University of Kansas

Nathaniel Wheelwright, Bowdoin College

Dean and Laurie Williams, Purdue University

Last, I would like to thank the many members of the Monteverde community whom I have not listed but who shared their lives with me and went out of their way to make me feel welcome.

Glossary

agricultural extension education, usually conducted by a public agency, directed at improving farming or other agricultural practices

amplexus the mating embrace of a frog or toad during which eggs are shed and fertilized

biodiversity or **biological diversity** a term that refers to the total number of species on Earth. Also refers to the variety of habitats on earth and genetic diversity within each species

brood a group of offspring

camouflage colors, shapes, or patterns that allow a living organism to blend in with its surroundings

canopy root a root originating in the branch of a tree, usually growing into a mat of epiphytes

diversity the different kinds or types of a group of things

echolocation the process by which bats and some other animals locate prey and other objects by emitting sounds and listening to their echoes

ecologist a biologist who studies natural communities of plants and animals

epiphylls plants that grow on the leaves of other plants

epiphytes plants that grow on top of other plants, especially on other trees

gaps openings in the forest canopy caused by fallen trees or other disturbances

gene pool the total sum of genetic diversity found in a species or population of organisms

host an organism whose body provides nourishment and shelter for a parasite; also refers to the tree upon which strangler figs and other epiphytes live

microcorridors strips of forest that connect two larger patches of forest

mutualistic an interaction between two species in which both species benefit

natural selection the process that "weeds out" unsuccessful genetic characteristics in a population of organisms, allowing those individuals with successful characteristics to survive and pass on their successful characteristics to their offspring; over time, this process can lead to the evolution of new species of plants and animals

nocturnal organisms that are active primarily at night

pheromone a chemical substance released by an organism into the environment as a specific signal to another organism, usually of the same species; they often function to attract mates

shade intolerant an attribute of a tree or other plant that means it can only grow in well-lit conditions

substrate the surface or layer, such as soil or moss, upon which an organism lives

tank bromeliads a certain group of plants—usually epiphytes—whose leaves form a central "cup" or "tank" that collects water, dust, and debris

tropical cloud forest a special type of tropical forest that grows at high altitudes where there is abundant precipitation

tropical montane forest *See tropical cloud forest*

Index

Page numbers in *italics* indicate illustrations.

About the Author

Sneed B. Collard III is the author of more than a dozen books about science, natural history, and the environment. In addition to traveling to Costa Rica to research *Monteverde*, he has journeyed to Asia, Australia, Europe, the Middle East, the Caribbean, and the South Pacific. When he is not writing or traveling, Sneed speaks to students and educators about writing, biology, and environmental protection. He currently lives in Missoula, Montana.

	DATE DUE		
DEC 0 1 1998			
MAY 0 2 2001			
SEP 0 5 2002			
JAN 2 6 2005			
AUG 0 8 2006			
MAY 0 1 2008			